Planning
Successful
Meetings
and Events

Planning Successful Meetings and Events

A Take-Charge Assistant Book

Ann J. Boehme

AMACOM
American Management Association
New York • Atlanta • Boston • Chicago • Kansas City • San Francisco • Washington, D.C.
Brussels • Mexico City • Tokyo • Toronto

This publication is designed to provide accurate and authoritative information in regard to the subject matter covered. It is sold with the understanding that the publisher is not engaged in rendering legal, accounting, or other professional service. If legal advice or other expert assistance is required, the services of a competent professional person should be sought.

Library of Congress Cataloging-in-Publication Data

Boehme, Ann J.
    Planning successful meetings and events / Ann J. Boehme.
        p.   cm.
    Includes index.
    ISBN 0-8144-7995-2
    1. Meetings—Planning.   I. Title.
HF5734.5.864   1998   98–35089
658.4′56—dc21   CIP

Printing number

10 9 8 7 6 5 4 3 2 1

I dedicate this book to my family: to my mother and father, who were living examples of the philosophy of Aristotle, as each taught me in their own way that one should always do the best you're capable of. And I dedicate this book to my daughters, Diane and Linda, who applauded all my small achievements and encouraged me "to do." Who would not be fueled by a glow in the eyes of children as they say: "Go for it, Mommy!"

My thanks to my family for their love and support.

Contents

Acknowledgments

I have been in this industry for more than twenty-three years, and I learn something every day. There is always a better way to accomplish a task, a better checklist to be made, a new glossary to be formed, more technology to be learned, more sophisticated software to be implemented—and there is always a benefit when I consult with a colleague. The most special reward or bonus, however, is that over the years, the numerous colleagues I have been privileged to meet and work with have become my very special friends.

Acknowledgments and much appreciation to my colleagues for their help with this book:

Ulla Buchner-Howard, CMP, UBH International, Inc.

Ruthe Davis, CMP, CHTTA, New York University

Dave Erickson, *Medical Meetings*

Muriel Jameson, The Telemarketing Institute

Virginia M. Lofft, Adams Business Media

Dan McCown, Independent Trade Show Consultant

Ronald J. Naples, CMP, Meeting Consultant

Mary Pekas, The Telemarketing Institute

James Spellos, American Management Association

Introduction

Meetings have been held throughout the centuries; although the venues have changed, much has stayed the same. Oratorical skills were appreciated, philosophies were presented, the word was spread, people met to learn, listen, and make assessments—and all that continues in meetings today. Then and now, educators introduce current issues to the masses. There were and are political meetings, business meetings, public meetings, religious meetings, social meetings, and more.

Meetings as we know them today embrace many forms. Any gathering, large or small, with goals, objectives, or a planned agenda constitutes a meeting. Meetings may take many months of preparation, or they may be called at a moment's notice.

Many of us are not aware that when we plan a meeting, we become part of the large number of people who operate within the parameters of what has become known as the meeting industry. The meeting industry is relevant and helpful to us today as it provides us with information, formal guidelines for planning meetings, resources, and benchmarks from which to operate.

Many years ago, as an executive secretary to the treasurer of a Fortune 500 company, I organized board meetings. At that time, no specific meeting planning association was in existence, nor were there publications to provide information and resources.

A few years later, professional meeting associations were established; an entrepreneur who saw the need also began producing meeting conferences. I recall clearly my first "industry meeting." It was a meeting for people with positions similar to mine: secretaries, nurses, and medical education coordinators who worked for medical centers; medical associations or physicians who were planning meetings for the physician community; and allied health professionals.

After three days of learning and networking at the University of San Antonio, I returned to my office where my vice president asked if his money had been well spent. He asked me to document three items that would indicate it was worthwhile for me to have attended the conference.

I was prepared, as I knew he would question me. I answered, "First, I learned there are others out there just like me, with the same responsibilities and the same problems, in need of solutions. Second, I learned that for those of us for whom planning meetings is not our only responsibility, there are simply not enough hours in the day; we need some assistance. Third, I learned that we really are doing everything right. Because I was working in a vacuum, I had no way to assess performance. Now I can assure you that we are on target and serving the needs of the medical center." What I was saying is that with a support system, you move along more securely.

In the area of time limitations, however, not much has changed in the past twenty years for anyone planning part or all of a meeting. Those of you who plan meetings less than 100 percent of the time wonder, How can I accomplish meeting tasks that will consume 100 percent of my time in addition to all my other responsibilities? You have many colleagues with the same question. I meet you every day and want to assure you that you are most likely doing a fine job. But you need to know that the nature of planning meetings is such that it can and will consume as much time as is available.

This book is meant to support you, to help you understand and introduce many functions of planning a meeting, to enable you to organize your time better, to provide you with resources and information to eliminate time-costly searches, and to guide you as you move through the large, diverse, and fun-filled environment of the meeting world.

I can't promise to stretch your day, decrease your responsibilities, or even provide you with masterful shortcuts. I can only promise that I will provide you with resources and information that will eliminate many questions and much guesswork, as well as contacts (through associations and publications) who have been there and can share with you the results of their experiences.

I hope this helps you plan more efficiently and keeps some of the fun in the function of planning part or all of a meeting.

Planning
Successful
Meetings
and Events

1

Planning a Meeting

What You Need to Know— What You Need to Do

There are various types of meetings, many different settings for each meeting, and many goals or objectives for conducting a meeting. The first major step will be gathering comprehensive information that will drive the development and organization of a plan to accomplish the many tasks at hand.

Who Plans Meetings?

From secretary to corporate president, everyone, in one way or another, has some involvement in planning meetings. Some plan meetings full-time, while countless secretaries and administrative assistants plan meetings on a part-time basis, as part of their overall responsibility. Whether there is full-time or part-time involvement, the end result—the meeting itself—must be perfection, as it professionally represents the sponsors and/or the corporation.

What's in a Title?

Your title may not reflect your meeting planning responsibility. You are in good company as many full-time planners have titles that do not indicate their true responsibilities either. Planners have many titles: secretary, executive secretary, meeting director, manager, marketing services manager, travel planner, director of travel management, administrative assistant, senior program consultant, program consultant, meeting planner, group travel coordinator, director of education, executive director, continuing education coordinator, director of continuing medical education, executive assistant, vice president of sales, vice president of education, project coordinator. Need I say more?

More than twenty-three years ago as a medical secretary, I completed planning my first series of medical meetings; my employer decided to change my title to that of continuing education coordinator. To support the change, he asked me to outline my responsibilities and the amount of time allocated to each of the stated responsibilities. Diligently every task was listed and my report submitted. My employer tossed it back and said, "No one could do all that you have listed! Please provide me with a more realistic list." I decided he was correct and that "No one could." So I asked for an assistant. After some serious negotiations, my request was granted and a new responsibility was added to my list, that of managing staff.

What Are the Responsibilities?

You will be asked to perform a variety of tasks. The duties noted make a point about the diversity of the meeting planner role. It is a widely accepted fact that anyone who plans meetings has multiple responsibilities, works long hours to accomplish the tasks, juggles many functions at once, has high energy, develops and relies on good interpersonal relationships, has excellent written and oral communications skills, is creative and almost overorganized, and—most important—is, or becomes, unflappable!

You will need to build on many of the skills you already have. Some of the most important and basic skills you will need as you plan meetings are to:

- Work well with others.
- Be detail-oriented.
- Function as a problem solver.
- Be a good negotiator.
- Be able to manage conference finances.
- Understand hotel operations.
- Plan effective menus.
- Effectively work with audiovisual (AV) companies.
- Be computer literate.
- Be well versed in international travel.

- Be able to entertain very important persons (VIPs) and international guests.
- Be able to take groups abroad and learn protocols.
- Have a dogged determination to get it done.

Duties (or Tasks)

- Identify needs and/or plan to meet the set needs and goals/objectives of a meeting.
- Develop agenda or meeting formats.
- Research sites and facilities.
- Select or recommend sites.
- Assess facilities.
- Arrange transportation.
- Coordinate activities of staff assigned to the meeting.
- Recruit and train staff and ad hoc personnel.
- Create workable budget or prepare to work within specified budget.
- Develop timelines.
- Inspect site and facility.
- Negotiate travel arrangements and hotel contracts.
- Negotiate with all related vendors (transport companies, destination management companies, tour guides, special event companies, AV companies)
- Locate printers.
- Provide mailers.
- Plan food and beverage functions.
- Negotiate prices.
- Interact with speakers and VIPs.

Who Holds Meetings?

Meetings are produced or sponsored by corporations, associations, universities, medical centers, and private seminar or conference companies. Corporations conduct meetings for their employees, their boards, and their shareholders. Associations produce annual meetings and educational meetings for their members or industry colleagues. Medical meetings are produced not only by associations (medical associations or professional academies) but also by companies dealing with medical products and by universities providing physicians and allied health professionals with continuing medical education. Major categories of meeting producers include religious, insurance, financial, technical, and others.

How Is an Attendee Notified of a Meeting?

Corporate meetings are usually mandated. Invitations or meeting notices may be forwarded via letter, memorandum, or newsletter using postal service, internal corporate system, fax, or E-mail.

Attendance at association meetings is generally solicited by direct mail (a flyer or brochure noting all pertinent data and requiring a fee to be returned along with a completed registration form). Even educational programs or seminars will charge a fee for attendance, although it may be nominal for association members.

Private seminar and meeting companies are in business to make a profit. They solicit via direct mail, telemarketing, broadcast, fax, Internet, E-mail, or whatever current marketing strategy works well and maximizes attendance at a meeting.

What Kinds of Meetings Are There?

There are various kinds of meetings and meeting designs. Before you consider which meeting format you will use, the first step is to identify and understand the event you will plan.

The meeting format should fit the meeting goals and objectives and be kept in mind as the selections of the city, site, and specific meeting rooms are under consideration.

The following identifies some of the popular meeting types and formats:

• The *board meeting*, which is composed of corporate board members, may be held on a regular basis in the corporate headquarters or designated boardroom. Company-specific policies will prevail for such meetings.

- The *sales conference* may be called to announce or kick off a sales product or sales period, such as a quarterly sales meeting, or it may be called to assess a past sales period and offer rewards and commendations.

- The *management meeting* is a corporate event that is held for executives; it may be in response to a corporate problem.

- A *corporate retreat* may be held for any number of reasons, including reinforcement of corporate policy, change in corporate policy, or assessment of performance.

- An *awards ceremony* may be developed for new research and development, outstanding product sales, a successful fund-raiser, capital development achievements, and sometimes a special morale booster.

- A *holiday party* will usually be held for corporate executives, their clients, and their services vendors.

- The *annual meeting* may be a shareholders' meeting in a corporation or the annual membership meeting for a trade association.

- The *product launch* introduces and promotes a new product to the professional community or the consumer.

- The *seminar* is a meeting designed to provide information, with discussion about that information. This is usually an interactive meeting with attendee participation and feedback.

- The *workshop* is a course that demonstrates and is designed to offer practical applications. It may be a hands-on workshop designed to improve a skill or a course that provides a setting for practice in a particular area.

- A *conference* is a meeting designed for discussion, consultation, and exchange of information, usually composed of general sessions and smaller group meetings to fact-find and solve problems.

- A *convention* is a large gathering of association members who convene for a specific purpose; it is usually composed of general sessions, committee meetings, and workshop sessions.

- *Incentive meetings* are rewards for performance; they may be for high-performance employees, distributors, or customers. As a business motivational tool, they are also thought to improve performance, to motivate consumers, and to motivate nonsales employees as well.

- The *general assembly* or *plenary session* is a gathering of all participants to listen to a keynoter and one or more presenters for a specific period of time—used at least once during a conference.

- *Concurrent sessions* are smaller sessions on different topics that are of interest to portions of the overall audience; these sessions are presented at the same time. *Breakout sessions* differ from concurrent sessions in that the topics of the small meetings are the same.

- *Training sessions* are usually held from a minimum of one day up to several weeks. These on-site, highly intensive interactive training sessions are led by professional trainers with specific expertise in one or more topics and must accomplish very specific, targeted goals.

- *Team-building events* by corporations provide sports and various challenges to build teams and specially constructed activities to demonstrate the importance of teams to select groups of employees. The goal is to change and shape and develop strong teams for the benefit of the corporate goals. The methods range from going white-water rafting to leading blindfolded team members through obstacle courses, but all involve working as a team against another team for a specific outcome.

- *Fund-raisers* are events designed for givers of monies for any number of philanthropic endeavors; traditionally, these are black-tie galas in upscale facilities, museums, concert halls, theaters, or opera houses. Other fund-raising events include golf and tennis tournaments.

- *Special events* include theme dinner parties; group tours; entertainment (for all, for spouses, or for kids before, during, or after the meeting), on premises or off premises (in theaters, on yachts, at the opera, at a concert, in museums, or at other historical venues); and golf or tennis tournaments.

Alternative Meeting Options

Teleconferencing allows information to be sent from one major meeting site to one or more "down-link" sites. The transmitting site can be corporate headquarters, a hotel, a conference center, or another facility with satellite or fibre-optic requirements.

Tele-suites are now offered by some hotel chains. These rooms (suites) may be rented on an hourly basis. Up to five executives may sit in one tele-suite location and be connected to another tele-suite in a distant city for a simulated roundtable meeting. The suites are identical or mirror setups.

Videoconferencing is a cost-effective way for corporations to disseminate current information (from one destination) to key players in different locations via one- or two-way video transmittal.

One-way audioconferencing is used for group communications, transmitting voice only from one site to one or more other sites. Two-way audioconferencing requires advance planning and a moderator who determines when the next speaker may be heard at the sites.

What Are the Meeting Planning Steps?

Goals and Objectives

Setting the goals and objectives of a meeting and providing a meeting agenda are the backbone of a meeting. The goals and/or objectives may be any of the following:

- To train
- To inform
- To educate
- To explore a concept
- To introduce something or someone
- To come to a decision
- To motivate
- To develop
- To display
- To support
- To improve
- To solve problems
- To learn how to make a profit
- To make a profit

Corporations have their unique policies and procedures and generally train new sales or executive employees to perform in accordance with their policies. Some training programs are lengthy and may be scheduled for thirty days or more in a conference setting. Other programs are held in remote locations or in the city where the new employees will operate. These are sometimes called orientation meetings.

When there is a research and development team, many corporations elect to discuss the new developments and plans behind closed doors, off corporate premises, in a think-tank environment such as a remote conference center.

When quarterly sales are down, so are spirits. Some meetings are designed to boost morale, and an upbeat educational environment may be sought.

When asked to plan a meeting, it's appropriate to pose a few questions of your own. You will want to ask your employer, the program sponsor, the developer, or the program chairman, Why do you want this meeting? What do you want to accomplish? Write one or two lines or a brief paragraph describing the meeting goals and the desired outcome of the meeting; review these with the program chairman. When you are both on the same page, you can proceed.

Next there follows a logical series of questions to be asked and addressed:

- What is the target date for this meeting?
- How many days will the meeting be?
- Where will the meeting be held?
- What is the meeting style or format?
- How much space does the meeting require?
- Has this meeting been run before? What were the results?
- How many people will be in attendance?
- Who is the target audience?
- What is the budget?
- Is this a rate-sensitive group?
- What quality hotel or facility is desired?
- What is the maximum room rate to be considered?
- How shall we contact the prospective audience?

- Who will produce the invitations or solicitations?
- Will there be printed educational materials?
- Will there be a printed program for distribution?
- Who are the speakers?
- How shall they be retained?
- What will the audiovisual requirements be?
- How many food and beverage events will there be?
- Will spouses and families attend as well?
- Will there be special activities for attendees? For attendees and families? For spouses and families?
- Who will pay for their activities?
- Will we be responsible for their transportation, or will travel be on their own?
- Will there be a fee for attendance?

What evolves from the questions is information that will form two valuable lists. You will have gathered information that will provide you with one list of all that must be accomplished and the targeted time for accomplishing the tasks; this list is your program timeline or timetable. You will also be able to put together a second list, a comprehensive list called meeting specifications (covered later in this chapter).

Program Timeline (Timetable)

Your timeline will become your guide. *Note:* The timeline should list any and all tasks in connection with the preparation, development, and execution of the meeting. Make it as comprehensive as possible for each meeting.

A simple timetable is shown in Figure 1-1.

A more complex or lengthy meeting might require a timeline such as the one in Figure 1-2.

Meeting Specifications

You are now ready to develop your meeting specifications, or meeting specs. The timelines are generally for your internal use, possibly to be shared and discussed with your meeting chairman or supervisor and staff. The meeting specs, however, will be forwarded to facilities and

Figure 1-1. Simple timeline.

Meeting name: _____   Meeting date: _____
Location: _____   Time: _____
Number of attendees: _____   Meeting objective/type: _____

Task		Target Date/Prior to Meeting
☐ Hold committee/staff meeting to solidify goals/meeting.	⇔	8 weeks prior
☐ Review budget.	⇔	
☐ Secure facility.	⇔	7 weeks prior
☐ Determine meeting format.	⇔	
☐ Review/obtain signed contract.	⇔	
☐ Develop program flyer, submit for approval.	⇔	
☐ Print meeting invitation.	⇔	6 weeks prior
☐ Obtain travel information; secure reservations.	⇔	
☐ Submit preliminary program materials for approval.	⇔	
☐ Distribute program invitations.	⇔	5 weeks prior
☐ Send program materials to designer.	⇔	
☐ Submit slide materials for approval.	⇔	
☐ Hire temp staff for on-site.	⇔	4 weeks prior
☐ Order gifts and amenities.	⇔	
☐ Secure AV.	⇔	
☐ Make travel arrangements for speakers/VIPs.	⇔	
☐ Confirm all attendees.	⇔	3 weeks prior
☐ Order all food and beverages.	⇔	
☐ Print posters.	⇔	
☐ Ship all materials to program.	⇔	2 weeks prior
☐ Send guarantees to hotel for meeting and food/beverage.	⇔	
☐ Rehearse on-site personnel.	⇔	1 week prior
☐ Review all confirmations.	⇔	
☐ Review all events.	⇔	
☐ Establish on-site presence.	⇔	Night before
☐ Hold preconference meeting with facility.	⇔	

other outsiders who will want to know your formalized meeting needs so they can provide you with services. The meeting specifications will be forwarded to hotels as requests for proposals (RFPs) that will include the meeting data you accumulated so they may bid on your piece of business.

If you require meeting space in a conference center, you can contact I.A.A.C. (the International Association of Conference Centers), and send an RFP via E-mail to all potential facilities. Call 314-993-8575 to obtain on-line information.

Your meeting specs may be simple, as for a dinner meeting or a holiday party, or they may be more lengthy if you are planning a full one- or two-day meeting. See Figure 1-3 for a sample meeting specifications form.

Your meeting specifications as noted in Figure 1-3 are for a simple meeting. The information is sufficient for a preliminary potential match and will give the hotels an opportunity to check their schedules to see if they have the available dates, in your price range, as well as the meeting-room space you require.

It will be important for them to know if you are flexible with your date options or not. You will also need to take into account the date of your request. If your meeting date options are close at hand, you may have more difficulty obtaining the needed space. You may be lucky, however, as small meetings sometimes fit well into a space that has been cancelled by another group. Such matches do occur from time to time.

For more complex meetings, you may prepare a cover sheet with the information noted above and also develop a comprehensive, hour-by-hour meeting agenda and schedule, which will outline the following information:

- Number of setup days (prior to meeting)
- Number of tear-down days (after meeting)
- Exhibit requirements
- Registration requirements
- Sleeping rooms for VIPs
- Hospitality suite requirements
- Number of staff rooms required
- Number and description of all food functions
- Number and description of special activities
- Transportation requirements
- Bell service for delivery of amenities
- Complete AV setup
- Handling of deposits
- Master account setup
- Requests for disclosure of renovation plans
- Requests for disclosure of competitive companies that may be scheduled in a facility at the same time of your meeting

Figure 1-2. Timeline for a complex meeting.

Meeting name: _____ Meeting date(s): _____
Location: _____ Time: _____
Number of attendees: _____ Meeting objective/type: _____

Task	16	15	14	13	12	11	10	9	8	7	6	5	4	3	2	1	0	1	2	3	4
		Weeks Before Meeting															Weeks After Meeting				
Initiate program.	↑																				
Define audience.	↑																				
Confirm date(s).		↑																			
Select destination.		↑																			
Select venue.			↑																		
Conduct site inspection.			↑																		
Secure contract/facility.			↑																		
Develop agenda.				↑																	
List subjects.				↑																	
Identify speakers.				↑																	
Solicit sponsors.					↑																
Solicit exhibitors.					↑																
Arrange special events.						↑															
Place advertisements.							↑														
Send press releases.			↑																		
Secure speakers.			↑																		
Order lists.			↑																		
Design invitations.				↑																	
Obtain print quote.				↑																	
Print announcements.				↑																	
Mail announcements.					↑																
Send announcements to exhibitors.					↑																
Send announcements to speakers.					↑																

Obtain speaker outlines/material.
Prepare workbook material.
Secure speaker/VIP travel.
Purchase amenities/gifts.
Confirm hotel arrangements.
Obtain slides from speakers.
Select all menus.
Secure AV company/arrangements.
Order signage.
Print meeting materials (workbook).
Rehearse on-site procedure.
Prepare name badges.
Prepare registration lists.
Prepare welcome letters.
Prepare evaluations.
Prepare certificates.
Ship materials to meeting site.
Arrive on site.
Have a preconference meeting.
Check slide review for speakers.
Assess meeting days.
Distribute gifts/certificates.
Assess evaluations.
Thank speakers.
Settle accounts.

Figure 1-3.   Sample meeting specifications form.

Meeting name (company): _____ Contact person: _____
Address: _____
Tel.: _____Fax: _____ E-mail: _____
Meeting type: _____ Meeting date(s): _____
1st choice date: _____ 2nd choice date: _____ 3rd choice date: _____
Estimated number of attendees: _____ Time of meeting: _____
Number of nights: _____ Number of rooms required: _____ Room type: _____
Range of acceptable room rates: _____
Food functions: 1. _____ 2. _____ 3. _____
Meeting room requirements: _____
Audiovisual requirements: _____
Additional requirements: _____
Group meeting history: _____

The more comprehensive your meeting specifications, the less opportunity there is for error or omission of an important meeting requirement. As your meeting progresses, you will also want to keep notations about your progress as reference for your next meeting.

Checklist—Planning a Meeting

☐ Information collected
☐ Name of the meeting
☐ Program chairman
☐ Goal/objective of the meeting
☐ Type of meeting
☐ Number of people attending
☐ Method of informing them of the meeting
☐ Fee for attendance
☐ Budget
☐ Date(s) it will be held
☐ Location where it will be held
☐ On premises
☐ Off premises
☐ Meeting hours

- ☐ Speakers
- ☐ Topics
- ☐ Meeting agenda
- ☐ Lectures
- ☐ Panel discussions with Q&A
- ☐ Case studies
- ☐ Small group discussions
- ☐ Concurrent sessions
- ☐ Workshops
- ☐ Meeting room requirements
- ☐ Food functions
- ☐ Breakfast
- ☐ Coffee breaks
- ☐ Luncheon
- ☐ Intermissions
- ☐ Reception
- ☐ Dinner
- ☐ Banquet
- ☐ Box lunch
- ☐ Materials for distribution at the meeting
- ☐ Exhibit area
- ☐ Meeting requirements

Glossary

agenda   A list of subjects to be discussed at a meeting.

association   An organization made up of people with common goals or in the same industry.

attendee   An individual who participates in a seminar, conference, trade show, or meeting.

breakout session   A spin-off group from a large meeting for discussion of specific subjects.

budget   Financial sheets that provide line items for each potential meeting expense.

concurrent sessions   Sessions scheduled at the same time.

conference   A meeting of people with similar interests for gathering and exchanging of information and networking.

conference centers   Facilities designed to provide sleeping and meeting rooms primarily for corporate use.

convention   A large assembly of trade or organization members.

corporate meetings   Various kinds of meetings for those who work for corporations.

fund-raisers   Events held specifically for the purpose of raising funds or capital development.

keynoter   A speaker who is the main attraction.

meeting specifications   All data acquired about a meeting.

panel discussion   Two or more speakers sitting at a table, facing the audience, and discussing issues.

plenary session   A main conference session with a speaker or speakers.

poster session   Participants submitting their work on preset poster sizes for display on corkboards in an exhibit area or other designated area during a meeting.

Q&A   A question-and-answer period.

RFP   A request for proposal.

timeline   A list and guide with specific target dates for execution of meeting tasks.

VIP   A very important person.

2

Site and Destination Selection

What are the considerations for selection of a facility and a destination? How will you set up a site selection critique? There is a logical progression to gathering information needed to implement a meeting: You gather information (1) about the program (meeting specifications), (2) about needed features at the site, and (3) about potential destinations with facilities with the needed features.

The meeting specifications (covered in Chapter 1) and information previously gathered will be forwarded to facilities and outside sources in the form of a request for proposal (RFP). Once you have completed your meeting specifications, the focus shifts to site selection. Your goal is to find a site that will be accepted as appropriate by the organizers and attendees alike.

Making Site Selection Checklists

Your next set of lists will be your site selection checklists, which will note all the important features you may require for your meeting. A carefully structured site selection checklist, noting good and bad hotel features, will provide a comprehensive assessment tool for comparison of various facilities.

In addition to physical appearance, available function rooms, food and beverage, and the ability to provide all amenities, there is the issue of management philosophy, which will impact on the service you and your group receive from a hotel. You may want to inquire about staff turnover, length of current ownership, and service policies. It would also be helpful to obtain a copy of a union contract (if the facility is a union hotel) and references from recent clients.

Selecting the Type of Meeting Site

The following list of potential meeting sites gives you an idea of the venues available to you. You should assess the options individually, based on the meeting format, the number of people expected to attend, an audience profile, and, most important, the meeting goals, objectives, and preferences (if known) of the attendees. Your question is simple: Where will the meeting needs be best served? Here are some meeting site options:

- Hotels (downtown hotel, suburban hotel, airport hotel, suite hotel)
- Resort facility
- Golf resort
- Gaming facility
- Cruise ship
- College or university facility
- Convention center
- Conference centers (executive conference center, corporate conference center, resort conference center, nonresidential conference center)

Hotel

If in a hotel, will a full-service hotel be best? Full-service hotels have appeal for groups preferring to keep the attendees on-site as everything is available under one roof. Mall hotels have a similar appeal. The services include a concierge, restaurants, various shops, a car rental desk, a health facility, and a business center. The high cost of running a full-service hotel has slowed construction of such facilities, but there are still large numbers of full-service hotels available for groups.

What is a limited-service hotel? Does this imply no service for the guest? No! Not at all. In fact, the term *limited-service hotel* is disputed as a misnomer. Generally, it is a facility where food and beverage service is limited (less than 10 percent of revenue is derived from the food and beverage service). For the planner, limited-service hotels do not provide large meeting rooms, large lobbies, on-site restaurants, room service, or bellmen to carry luggage. They do provide excellent lodging, however, for rate-sensitive attendees or those caught in an overflow situation.

Conference and meeting hotels (those with function space for the meetings) are geared to serve groups, and a dedicated convention services manager (CSM) will be assigned to work with the contact person (the planner). After the sale, the account is turned over to the CSM. The role of the CSM is to service the account, to adhere to the terms of the contract, and to make it happen. A good CSM is dedicated to your meeting.

Hotel facilities accommodate large and small groups, have one or more ballrooms, 24-hour staffing, and ample resources to make it work. Their prices vary considerably from city to city and region to region; season has a heavy impact on price. Value dates should be discussed. (Value dates are dates when the hotel traditionally has less than a full house and wants business. The room rates are lower during this period.)

Downtown Hotel

The distance from the airport (including traffic impact on drive time) needs to be considered when selecting a downtown hotel. If a number of participants are local, this may be the wise choice. In many instances, the city is the attraction, along with nearby shops, malls, restaurants, and extra activities. A downtown hotel with numerous amenities and conference facilities in a desirable city is a popular choice for meetings as spouses have numerous built-in activities at hand. Some hotels have a reputation for superior service. This reputation helps make them an attractive site.

Suburban Hotel

Suburban hotels may not be as attractive to fly-in groups. The transportation time from the airport to the facility and a residential atmosphere are more limiting. However, for local drive-in groups, these facilities are very popular.

Airport Hotel

Many busy executives elect to fly into a city and meet at the convenient airport hotel. You will find these facilities heavily booked Mondays through Fridays and very available on weekends for other types of meetings (including private parties, weddings, and social events).

Suite Hotel

Suite hotels have more comfortable living accommodations for longer meetings; they are, however, short on amenities such as room service, concierge, health facility, and business center.

Resort Facility

You have all been to resorts when you were a child that provided family getaways. Many corporate-style resorts are patterned after these resorts, and many have constructed conference meeting facilities to entice the corporate or meeting business to their property. Resort facilities may be a getaway nestled in the hills, an attractive summer destination on the water, or a winter ski resort in the mountains. They all provide opportunity for a meeting, fine dining, and built-in activities that are usually indicative of their region and season.

Golf Resorts

Some resorts are specifically for one sport, such as golf. If a group of executives or award winners will be participating in a golf tournament, a golf resort is the location of choice. Many such resorts are in the South, the Southwest, and California. Pebble Beach is one that comes to mind, even to those of us who are nongolfers. The benefits of a meeting at a golf resort are that the resort is completely set up to accommodate such a meeting, and staff is of great help to the organizers.

Gaming Facility

Las Vegas has become more and more popular as a meeting destination. Currently the city of Las Vegas is known for the mega-meetings of thousands, with the accompanying trade shows. The current home of the mega-meeting, Las Vegas is beginning to solicit and value the smaller meeting as well.

Cruise Ship

Cruise ships seem to be the most luxurious of prizes for award and incentive meetings. Built-in activities, extraordinary service, nonstop dining, and impeccable accommodations are the norm.

College or University Facility

College or university facilities can be very cost-effective; however, most universities will limit facility availability to time periods when they are not in session and the campus is empty.

Convention Center

Meeting size has a strong impact on site selection. Hotels have appeal as they offer a great deal of flexibility and can easily adjust to various meeting sizes. However, when a meeting outgrows a hotel facility due to size, the logical move is to a convention center. There are growing numbers of convention centers that house large conventions and trade shows. However, the number of cities nationwide that can house many thousands of attendees is still limited. These cities—such as Las Vegas, New York, Chicago, Dallas, Atlanta, Los Angeles, San Francisco, Orlando, and New Orleans—are in great demand as they have enough rooms available to accommodate large meetings, which will be presented in the convention centers.

New and under-construction convention centers are equipped with leading-edge technology. Sophisticated multimedia communications systems and fiber-optic wiring are now installed in the new convention centers and provide technological benefits, such as Internet hookups and kiosks where attendees can access E-mail. Videoconference capabilities and distance learning provide the option to communicate from the show floor or meeting rooms with colleagues and business associates in other cities.

Convention centers, by their sheer size, are intimidating. But as mega-meetings demand the space, they are in short supply, as are the cities that can house meetings of this magnitude.

For the meeting that has outgrown a hotel but is not yet a mega-meeting, there are medium-size convention centers that welcome their business. These centers accommodate thousands of attendees and are geared to the meeting business that does not have over-whelming space requirements. Many such convention centers have a hotel on the property, and surrounding areas also provide hotel accommodations as well as entertainment complexes.

A previous problem with convention centers, which seems to be working itself out, was the food and beverage quality. Catering functions are much better (in terms of quality and service) and continue to improve steadily. Be conservative when developing food and beverage menus; keep it simple because you are dealing in volume. For a convention of 10,000, it is not unusual to serve 12,000 to 15,000 hamburgers or 50,000 cups of coffee; for a two-day program, no less than 20,000 entrees will be served. That puts it in perspective.

Leasing space from a convention center is similar to renting an apartment. Generally, you lease four bare walls and have to decorate and build the insides. Apartments have fixed walls; convention centers do not. The main issues with growth and the move from a hotel facility to a convention center are the additional cost for leasing and the different-style contracts.

Another hurdle is the lack of pricing standards. There are no standard policies from convention center to convention center, and the buyer must be cautious and diligent with a checklist before a contract is signed. Not only is pricing inconsistent, but there are those convention centers that will book a decade ahead and make commitments while other convention centers will not discuss pricing unless the time frame is a year or less.

The leap from hotel to convention center is one that requires research and an adjustment in thinking as well as long-range planning.

Conference Center

Conference centers are an excellent setting for intensive training seminars, board meetings, sales and marketing presentations, team-building sessions, research and development brainstorming activities, introduction to changes in corporate policies, advanced adult education programs, and new employee orientation.

The unique selling position of conference centers is that they provide a dedicated learning atmosphere. They are geared to productive meetings that accomplish the goals and objectives of the client.

Packaging and pricing are two of the major differences between conference centers and hotels. The complete meeting package (CMP) is a tangible asset for the planner as it can relieve the planner of some of the logistical problems, leaving more time to concentrate on the agenda, speakers, and goal setting.

In a conference center, the CMP includes (on a per-night basis) sleeping accommodations, meeting space (including prefunction areas used for registration or refreshments), full American plan food service (breakfast, lunch, and dinner), continuous food and beverage service for coffee breaks and intermissions, plus basic audiovisual equipment and, in many instances, complete use of the facility (including spa, pool, table tennis, tennis, and other light gaming activities).

Though high-tech equipment is readily available, there may be a charge for equipment beyond the basics. The basic equipment will generally include screen, projectors, pointers, and audio. If the meeting requires advanced technology (such as videoconferencing, teleconferencing, or multimedia presentations), it is wise to price-check the CMP. Some conference centers offer more in their basic package than others.

The International Association of Conference Centers (IACC) has approximately 300 members in 13 countries. Members are corporate or executive conference centers, universities and college centers, and firms providing products and services to centers. The IACC monitors legislative developments affecting conference centers and sets basic standards for conference centers. The following standards assure those of us planning meetings that certain basic professional requirements are met:

- The meeting rooms should be available to the group on a 24-hour basis.
- The design of the chairs and space allotted for seating should be comfortable for not less than six hours.
- Acoustics and lighting should be supportive of the learning needs.
- Hard walls (not dividers) should separate the rooms, and the walls should provide surfaces that permit use of flip-chart sheets and other learning aid devices.
- The sleeping accommodations should provide an arrangement for working on evening assignments (homework).

Types of Conference Centers

Conference centers may be executive, corporate, resort, or nonresidential. The executive conference center has anywhere from seventy-five to a few hundred guest rooms and a large number of conference rooms; it is usually in a remote location. Many of these centers were converted from existing estates. Corporate conference centers are the largest conference center facilities; they may have up to 400 rooms and a substantial amount of conference space for training programs. Some large companies own their own corporate conference centers. Resort conference centers have extensive recreational activities, as well as areas for creative banquet and entertainment activity. Nonresidential conference centers have no guestrooms or recreation and only provide limited dining.

Matching the Meeting to the Facility

Training sessions succeed best in an environment geared specifically to adult learning, with staffing and enhancements set to achieve these specific goals. Ideal sites are the corporate conference center and resort facility. Research and development meetings need the security of a think tank. In many instances, the conference center or secluded retreat serves the purpose best. The association annual meeting site is usually selected in response to the opinions of the members; location preference and current popularity of a site impact strongly on the destination decision. Hotels geared for conferences are extremely suitable. Additional considerations are the size of the association and whether there will be exhibits in addition to the educational sessions. The incentive meeting must be upscale and nothing less than spectacular; the goal is to provide a reward for extraordinary performance. For trade and new product introduction, sites with exhibit space will be required, and easy access into and out of the city as well as the facility becomes an issue.

Selecting a Destination

Once you have decided on the type of facility you need, you must choose a destination. The best place to begin is with a call to the Convention and Visitors' Bureau in the city or cities noted as possible sites. Ask for a copy of their specific meeting planner guide. Many CVBs are on-line; check their Web site as well.

The local Convention and Visitors' Bureau will provide you with the names of suppliers, such as hotels, travel agencies, restaurants, and ground operators (those who will transfer your meeting participants from the airport to the facility), but it will not make assessments as to performance or recommend one over another. It is important to stress that the CVB will research facility availability and even make the introductions; the CVB will not, however, negotiate on your behalf.

You will also want to research facilities in the compiled periodic resources and property directories (such as *GAVEL* and *Official Meeting Facilities Guide*). These publications provide access to convention centers, hotels, and resorts in the United States and around the world. They will give you information about the following:

- Administration—Names and telephone numbers of sales directors and convention services departments; the address and current general manager in a facility
- Rates—Group room rates and seasonal room rates
- Accommodations—Number of rooms and suites, spa, fitness center, restaurants, other accommodation attractions
- Meeting rooms—Number of meeting rooms, room sizes, room configurations, meeting room diagrams

- Location—Near an airport, downtown facility, or resort
- Local transportation—Taxi service availability, shuttle service, proximity to airports
- Area maps—Near malls or activities
- Recreation—On-property recreation available, such as golf or tennis

Additional Resources and Facility Guides

Some major hotel chains have a guide listing their own facilities. Call any Marriott Hotel sales office and request a copy of the *MARRIOTT Meeting Planners Guide*, the ITT Sheraton North American Division for a copy of its *North American Meeting Facilities Guide*, and the Crowne Plaza Hotels & Resorts for its *Meeting Facilities Guide*.

Industry associations—such as Meeting Professionals International (MPI), American Society of Association Executives (ASAE), and Professional Convention Management Association (PCMA)—are additional supplier/vendor sources.

Selecting a Facility

The cities or destinations have been tentatively identified; you must now check to see if they have available space that meets your requirements and your target dates. Your focus is on a facility in a city or destination that can meet your needs. You are now ready to send your request for proposal (RFP) to the Convention and Visitors' Bureaus; you may also send an RFP to hotels you have identified and are interested in pursuing.

The CVB will check all facilities that match your RFP and advise you of space and date availability. At this time, the facilities selected to receive your RFP should also answer some questions. You will want to know what their forecast for occupancy is at the time of your meeting. Will the facility be in a sold-out mode, or will it be the low season, with only 45 percent or 50 percent occupancy forecast?

This is where the exchange between planner/organizer and the facility becomes so important. If each understands the other's needs and goals, the process moves quickly, and there are fewer misunderstandings to deal with later.

When a facility in an acceptable city or destination is available, an offer will be made to you that (1) outlines all space you will rent, rooms to be held and sold to your group, rates for the rental of conference space, dates of arrival and departure—in short, it will include all items noted on your RFP—and (2) includes a tentative letter of agreement or a more formal contract for your approval and agreement.

You are now ready to either accept the terms or wait until you have made a site visit. If you are familiar with the property or if your company will accept the property without a site inspection, you are ready for the contract.

If you are to make a personal site inspection tour, you will now prepare your checklists. There are no set systems for checklists. The most important issue is to be certain all items are listed. Check the ones relevant to the particular meeting, venue, and needs.

The Site Visit

Before considering a site visit, there should be acceptance and agreement to the meeting specifications, the facility should rank high and qualify as a prime candidate, and the contract should be generally acceptable.

If the site inspection is conducted in one's own city, there is more flexibility as travel and time are not issues. The decision to fly to another city or even out of the country for a site inspection generally indicates much preliminary site inspection has been conducted, and barring any totally unacceptable issues that might arise, this property will be the venue of choice.

The Office Site Inspection

Not all planners travel to destinations (whether domestic or international) for a site inspection tour. Unquestionably, the on-site visit has value: It provides the opportunity to assess the condition of a facility, its cleanliness, and the implementation of service policies; it also offers organizers a chance to develop relationships with the hotel sales and convention offices with whom they will work as the meeting develops.

However, the Internet is making some rapid changes (although the value of "armchair" or Internet site inspections remains to be seen and judged). For those who will conduct telephone, fax, and/or E-mail and Internet site visits, the checklist is even more important. It is critical to obtain very recent references as well as the assessments of previous clients, suppliers, and industry colleagues. (These must be colleagues with the same standards as you and those you represent.) The reputation of the facility must be impeccable. A site inspection videotape is also helpful. Here are the prerequisites for office site inspection:

- Prepare checklists.
- Do your homework—research property status.
- Check outcomes of other clients.
- Verify ownership. (Is the facility a brand-name facility but owned by a bank or other company? If so, when was the new ownership established?)
- Ask for disclosure regarding staff turnover rates. (Facilities with solid management generally have low turnover rates; turnover will have an impact on service.)
- Ask for a set of all printed menu offerings.
- Obtain scale drawings of the meeting areas, including registration area and/or foyer.
- Visit by video if possible.
- Collect data from suppliers.
- Determine current physical condition and turnover rates.
- Verify dates that the last renovations (upgrades of facility) took place.
- Ask about plans for the next renovation.
- Determine the policy for ongoing renovation.
- Verify the style of the facility, including grade of its clients/ guests.
- Determine its reputation for service.
- Find out if they are recipients of a recent service award.

- Ask about the occupancy pattern.
- Check on plans to sell/merge.

The Site Inspection Tour

There are five basic rules for setting up the site visit:

1. Meet with a decision maker. This makes it possible to resolve potential deal-breaking issues.
2. Whenever possible, conduct the site inspection during the dates suggested by the facility. It is not wise to visit when the facility is in a sold-out period as your visit then becomes a direct cost for the facility.
3. Never extend the site inspection for personal reasons; leave the family home.
4. Decide if it is better to arrive unannounced as a regular guest, to assess the general response to guests, or as an expected VIP to determine their treatment of VIPs.
5. Prepare for a backup facility in the event negotiations break down. However, never use one facility as leverage against the other; all prices as quoted rates should be considered confidential.

To reiterate, requirements for a good site inspection are good timing, prudent use of host hospitality (two nights for a domestic visit), preparation of a comprehensive checklist, a substantial reference check and recommendations, and at least one backup facility as an option.

Air Travel

When considering a destination and site, it is important to bring the air travel portion of the meeting into the equation. If flights are difficult or untimely, the destination may not be suitable. The airports and available ground transportation are important factors. You should be especially cautious when considering a remote resort facility. Ask the following questions:

Flights

- What is the frequency of scheduled flights to the destination?
- Are there sufficient connections for the traveler?

- Is there an off-season, which will affect the number of scheduled flights?
- Will the attendees travel as a group or travel individually?
- Who will book the travel?
- What is the distance from airports?
- Is train service available to the facility?
- What are airfares?
- What is the potential for upgrades and amenities?

Airports

- Is it a modern airport?
- Is it lively and efficient?
- Is it easy to navigate?
- What is the distance from the carrier to the baggage area?
- Is signage sufficient?
- Is the airport staff helpful, friendly, courteous, and knowledgeable (for large or small airports)?

Ground Transportation/Airport Convenience

- Are drivers and representatives of special transports permitted at the gate or in the baggage area to give VIP transfer treatment when needed?
- Does the baggage area operate smoothly?
- Are car services and shuttles readily available and staffed to provide traveler information?
- How much time does it take to depart from the carrier and arrive at the transfer vehicle?
- What are the distance and the travel time from the airport to the property?
- Would the transfer be at rush hour or at an off-peak time?
- Are there alternative routes?
- Are safety factors considered?

Familiarization (Fam) Trips

A familiarization trip is different from a site inspection tour inasmuch as site visits are supported by a facility of choice when a planner is considering booking that facility. Fam trips are generally offered by suppliers (publications on behalf of a supplier or advertiser, hotels, airlines, destination management companies, tourist boards, and/or Convention and Visitors' Bureaus, as well as any special venues such as cruise ships, museums, historical sites, and specialty restaurants). They ultimately translate into a real opportunity to thoroughly experience a destination for those who select meeting sites.

Fam trips are designed to showcase the destinations, the facilities, and the services. Strong supplier partnerships exist; the client is included in that partnership when a destination is booked. Once business is accomplished, the sellers have huge resources and provide their services to ensure a successful outcome.

During a fam trip, the planner will do the following:

- Test numerous facilities.
- Observe the climate of the destination.
- Assess the travel options (including transfer process).
- Sample the food and beverages.
- Experience the performance of destination management companies.
- Benefit from the creativity of the events planners as they suggest options for that location.
- Test and time the tours.
- Develop working relationships with critical and potential key partners for future meetings and events.

Planners and meeting organizers invited on fam trips are usually decision makers or those who make the recommendations to the decision makers in the areas of destination and lodging facility. In order to maximize the potential business for a destination or property, fam trip invitees are carefully screened and evaluated. In the interest of professionalism and ethics, one should only accept the invitation to be part of a fam trip if a booking in that destination is possible and if the attendee is either truly a decision maker or in the position of making a strong recommendation.

Site Inspection Costs

Flight arrangements and food and beverage are your responsibility. Generally it can be expected that the facility will host a lunch or dinner.

Airlines and group travel agencies will provide site inspection assistance. The airline of choice will either offer a discounted site inspection ticket or reimburse you for the ticket later if a booking results from the site inspection. This policy changes periodically; it is recommended that you check with the airline of choice for the current policy.

If possible, arrive the evening before a scheduled morning appointment. This provides an opportunity to visit the hotel on your own.

Checklist—Selection of Destination

- ☐ Sufficient hotel selection
  - ☐ Budget to luxury hotels available
- ☐ Nearby hotel available for overflow situation
- ☐ Event sites
- ☐ Tour options
- ☐ Airport access
- ☐ Flight availability to destination
- ☐ Sufficient restaurants
- ☐ Local shopping
- ☐ Nearby attractions

Checklist—Hotel Services Available

Category of Facility

- ☐ Downtown full-service hotel
- ☐ Airport hotel
- ☐ Resort hotel
- ☐ Suite hotel
- ☐ Suburban hotel
- ☐ Conference center

Hotel/Facility Services

- ☐ Parking
  - ☐ For fee
  - ☐ Free

- ☐ Car/shuttle service
  - ☐ To and from airport—complimentary
  - ☐ To and from airport—for fee
- ☐ Car rental desk
- ☐ Concierge
  - ☐ Manager on Duty (MOD) at all times
- ☐ Health club
- ☐ Pool
  - ☐ Indoor
  - ☐ Outdoor
- ☐ Ocean bathing
- ☐ Complete ADA facilities
- ☐ Golf
  - ☐ On premises
  - ☐ Nearby
  - ☐ Putting green
- ☐ Tennis
  - ☐ On premises
  - ☐ Nearby
- ☐ Restaurants
  - ☐ Convenient hours
- ☐ Room service
  - ☐ Hours
- ☐ Teleconferencing capabilities (audio and video)

Checklist—When on Your Own
Arrival at the Property

- ☐ Courteous reception by the staff
- ☐ Ease of registration/check-in
- ☐ Manager on duty
- ☐ Sufficient elevator banks
- ☐ Signage—access to meeting rooms

Season Compatibility—Group in Hotel

☐ Peak season (overly crowded or able to handle it)

☐ Off-season (still attractive or lose charm)

Facility and Room Assessment

☐ Lobby activity—is it lively?

☐ Facility newness—is it modern?

☐ Is it attractive, spotless, and well maintained?

☐ How are the standard rooms (same as group will have)?

☐ What is the location of the rooms—over garage, facing courtyard?

☐ Are there amenities such as bathrobes, TV remote controls, local events information?

☐ Does each room have adequate safety features on door?

☐ Are the fire instructions clear?

☐ Is there a sprinkler system?

☐ Is there a room safe?

Service in the Restaurant

☐ Variety of selections on menu and prices

    ☐ Excellent

    ☐ Good

    ☐ Adequate

☐ Hours restaurant is open

☐ Service and adequate staffing

☐ Quality of food

☐ Prices of alcoholic beverages and wine

    ☐ In restaurant

    ☐ In lounge

    ☐ In bar

☐ Lounge/bar

☐ Well-placed lounge/bar

Room Service

- ☐ Menu
- ☐ Service
- ☐ Prices
- ☐ Hours of service

Amenities

- ☐ Turndown service
- ☐ Radio for wake-up call
- ☐ Fax machine in room
- ☐ Other business equipment
- ☐ Efficiency of operator wake-up call
- ☐ Newspaper delivered to room in A.M.
- ☐ Automatic TV checkout

Checklist—The Official Site Inspection Tour to Review With Sales

Public Space

- ☐ Efficient and suitable, with normal activity
- ☐ Concierge—placement, efficiency
- ☐ Bell stand and storage—aid group arrivals and departures
- ☐ System for staffing registration desk during peak periods
- ☐ Private foyer or area for group preregistered check-in

Sleeping Rooms

- ☐ Number of rooms
- ☐ Number of suites
- ☐ Hospitality-type suites
- ☐ Presidential or penthouse suites
- ☐ Number of floors
- ☐ Quality and condition of rooms

☐ Concierge or business floor
☐ Rack rates of rooms
☐ Room categories—breakdown in block

Function Space

☐ Location–space configurations
☐ Scale drawings of all space
☐ Number of ballrooms
☐ Number possible for other bookings at same time
☐ Size of ballroom(s) (including ceiling height)
☐ Options for breakout rooms
☐ Number of air walls—soundproof or not
☐ Lighting flexibility—dimmers in each ballroom section
☐ Registration Area or Foyer
☐ Space for exhibits (how many can be accommodated)
☐ Location of freight elevators for exhibit and equipment movement
☐ Location of kitchen
☐ Available areas for food functions
☐ Terrace/outdoor garden
☐ Balcony
☐ Alternate sites
☐ Main corridors for access to kitchen and freight
☐ Telephone banks, elevators, escalators, coatroom, and rest rooms
☐ Availability of a dedicated room to house the show office
☐ Parking and access to ballrooms
☐ Access to package room

Food and Beverage

☐ All menus (dated if possible)
☐ Adequate room for food functions
☐ Easy access to the kitchen
☐ Types of service generally provided
☐ General scheduled facility theme parties
☐ Visiting the kitchen facilities

☐ Meeting the chef

☐ Plus/plus rates (how much gratuity/service and tax?)

☐ Coffee per gallon (mugs or cups)

☐ Bar prices

Audiovisual/Technical Items

☐ Is there an on-site AV company?

☐ What services do they provide?

☐ Can you obtain a comprehensive price list?

☐ Does AV have an office in-house?

☐ Must you use the in-house company?

☐ Is there a penalty if you bring your own company?

☐ What technological advancements has the hotel made?

  ☐ Audioconference?

  ☐ Teleconference?

  ☐ Videoconference?

  ☐ ISDN lines?

  ☐ Fiber optics?

Checklist—To Discuss While On-Site

☐ All contract items

☐ Sleeping rooms

☐ Function space

☐ Space in facility

☐ Ballroom configurations

☐ Assignment of dedicated convention services manager

☐ Food and beverage prices

☐ Union/labor contracts

☐ Hotel policies

☐ Services available

☐ Occupancy reports

☐ Plans for renovation

☐ Meeting profile and specifications

☐ Contract terms (review)

☐ Traffic flow and signage requirements

☐ AV requirements

☐ Schedule of preconvention meeting

☐ Transportation

☐ Americans With Disabilities Act (ADA) compliance

☐ BMI compliance

Glossary

agenda   An outline of the subject or subjects to be discussed at a meeting.

association   An organization of people with the same mission or agenda.

attendee   Anyone attending a meeting, conference, or convention.

breakout sessions   Small groups.

certified meeting professional (CMP)   A professional designation given by the CLC (Convention Liaison Council—Body of Meeting Associations).

complete meeting package (CMP)   An all-inclusive per-person price at a conference center.

concierge   Special staff providing special services to facility guests.

concurrent sessions   Sessions about different topics given at the same time.

conference   A meeting to disseminate information.

convention   A meeting of members of an association.

convention center   A large building designed to house large meetings.

Convention and Visitors' Bureau (CVB)   An organization designed to promote a destination and provide services for meetings.

high season   When a facility has highest occupancy and demand.

housing bureau   A service under the aegis of the CVB to provide housing for large groups.

incentive meeting   A meeting designed to award attendees for performance.

low season   When the facility has low occupancy (off-season).

MOD   Manager on duty in a hotel or facility.

overflow   A situation arising from sold-out pattern in a hotel.

panel   A group of speakers guided by a moderator for a presentation.

plenary session   The main session in a conference with full attendance.

sales meeting   A meeting of sales and marketing personnel; may be for product introduction or assessment of sales.

seminar   A lecture, including sharing information.

shoulder season   Moderately active season, between high season and low season.

site inspection   An inspection of the facility prior to booking.

teleconference   A meeting of people in two or more locations through a telecommunications system.

training session   An intensive learning experience with specific goals.

venue   The facility or meeting location.

workshop   Similar to a training session; usually hands-on to develop a skill.

3

Contracts

The Contract

What is a contract? A contract is an offer outlining specific terms that are accepted and agreed to by two or more rational parties, usually within a specified time. After the meeting specifications (dates, rates, space) have been reviewed and verbally agreed to (and when possible, a site visit accomplished), then a contract outlining each detail of the meeting will be forwarded. This contract will be reviewed; if all terms set forth are in accord with the buyer's needs and wants, it will be signed, dated, and returned to the facility.

Contracts may be simple two-page (short-form) documents or, for more complex and large meetings, lengthy (no-page-limit) documents with extremely comprehensive terms and conditions outlined. Contracts have become more complex, more rigid, and more legal than in the past. I can remember when letters of agreement, as well as verbal agreements, were a solid commitment. Of course, this is no longer the case. The norm today is lengthy, formal contracts, which outline every issue imaginable and protect the facility against any possibility of loss of revenue.

While you are not expected to be a lawyer, you will have to review contracts, make recommendations, and, in many instances, sign the formal document (as a representative of the company). Today, especially for the beginning or intermediate planner (and even the seasoned planner), it is advisable to seek the assistance of the corporation attorney, the association attorney, or independent counsel. In most instances, an officer would sign the contract with input from the planner and counsel.

Win/win negotiations are better accomplished when both parties understand the other's requirements, budget restrictions (of the buyer), and profit structure (of the supplier).

Over the past two decades, the pendulum has swung from somewhat balanced contracts to those favorable for the buyer to those favorable for the supplier. Whatever the current picture, parties negotiating contracts are locked into the present economic picture and must adjust to the buyer/supplier demand situation.

Today the lodging industry is high-occupancy/high-demand; that creates high room rates and puts the suppliers in the driver's seat. Will it change? It probably will. But much depends on whether there will be significant new construction of hotels, continuing buyouts and mergers of large hotel chains (which lessen competition), and availability of alternate facilities. Of course, the economic climate will vary from destination to destination.

There are five trends that have an impact on negotiations:

1. There is a lack of new full-service hotels.
2. Conference centers are more in demand than previously.
3. Hotels are after the leisure business, which is growing significantly due to the senior market.
4. Time-share business and vacation clubs are good business.
5. The meeting and conference business is not the number one market being sought by suppliers.

As meetings and conferences are not the prime market that hotel salespeople are targeting, they may hold off making a commitment regarding space in the hope that they can make more money selling their rooms to one of the more lucrative markets. This diminishes our ability to negotiate as we are not dealing from a position of strength.

Contracting With Hotels

Hotels have a scorecard and use it to evaluate your business. When you call and/or send your meeting specifications in search of a facility, they assess your need for space in conjunction with the number of sleeping rooms required and whether you can pay the rate they want for that room block. If your group is rate-sensitive, it might only fit into the picture during a low-season or low-demand period. If you have a low score, they may not want to consider your group. They would prefer to wait for a piece of business from another group.

This is a seller's market, and hotels want the right guest, at the right time, for the right price. What does that mean? It means hotels want to maximize revenue. Hotels are in business to generate revenue. The sale of rooms is their prime product, and it is a perishable and inelastic product. An unsold room on any given night is lost revenue that is not recoverable. Hotels want meeting-room space booked and every sleeping room sold at the maximum rate.

Food and beverage, as the second-largest revenue stream in a hotel, ranks high on the scoreboard. The more high-end meal functions you need, the better your score.

If a group or meeting has a history (has been conducted before)—and past results can be documented as to number of attendees, number of rooms used, amount of money spent, and timely or untimely payment—the facility will use that history to assist in making a decision for the forthcoming event.

A group's history scores in three areas:

1. Previous commitments and resultant room pickup.
2. Payment history. (Be certain to pay within thirty days if the contract required it. In the event of a dispute, pay the major portion of the bill and only retain the disputed amount until the situation is resolved.)
3. Potential for return business.

What kind of business do you represent? Are you an association, a corporation, a travel agent, or a seminar company? Do you want space during a peak period (high season)? Are the arrival and departure compatible with the hotel's need? These issues are all carefully assessed; the best piece of business will get the space. Once there is a match, the hotel will forward a contract for your review and acceptance.

Contracting With Convention Centers

For those who have not dealt with a convention center previously, it is wise to obtain some industry consultation concerning current practices. As with hotels, it is important to inquire about ownership. Is the convention center owned by the city, by the state, or privately? Are they partnering with hotels? Is their objective to break even or earn a substantial return on investment?

Ask if there is an exclusive agreement with vendors. If so, the agreement should be fully disclosed. Find out who has authority to make concessions for your piece of business. Only a year ago, I needed an alternate facility in a major convention city. The convention center was an option. I was surprised to learn of the exceptionally low rental fees, which were due to the financial structure of that facility. The ownership and financial obligations play a considerable part in the inconsistencies.

Purpose and Content of a Contract

In general, good contracts protect both parties. Preparation begins when the buyer first considers and approaches a property with needs and group requirements. Providing a hotel or facility with a list of required specifications for the meeting moves the process rapidly, with less chance for miscommunication.

What should be in a contract? Everything! Don't be misled into believing it is better not to address a sticky issue. In the event of a dispute, the courts do not look favorably on the omission of a clause that would have stated terms, conditions, and agreement to those terms. It is only when terms are stated that the interests of both parties are served.

Usually the party who writes the contract has the upper hand. Difficult issues or contracts written in legalese may require review by an industry lawyer.

Forty-One Clauses You Should Be Aware Of

Clauses that should be in a contract include but are not limited to the following forty-one items:

1. *Room block/room rates.* These are specific numbers indicating how many rooms are needed each night and the rate for the stated rooms.

2. *Complimentary rooms.* A specific policy states the number of complimentary rooms allocated to the group each night (room nights). Hotels have traditionally provided one complimentary room for every fifty booked (per night).

3. *Staff rooms/rates.* These are the discounted rates and allocation of rooms for the staff; they vary based on the number required and the total group business.

4. *Suites and/or VIP upgrades.* Specific requirements should be listed.

5. *Room locations.* The specific sleeping room locations and quality of rooms rented should be noted.

6. *Run of the house.* One specific room rate is available for a variety of rooms, usually with an equal percentage of rooms in each category for the one adjusted, average rate.

7. *No-walk clause.* This is sometimes called an overflow clause. While this is no real guarantee that group members (even those with a credit card guarantee) will not be walked to another hotel in the event of overbooking, it is a good safety net.

8. *Short-stay penalties.* If a group has been blocked for 100 people from Wednesday through Saturday and some leave prior to the last night blocked, penalties may be imposed because those rooms are unfilled and revenue loss occurs.

9. *Check-in/checkout.* The specific times for check-in/checkout are based on hotel policy.

10. *Early check-in/late checkout.* If a deviation from the hotel policy is needed, be certain it is noted in the contract.

11. *Reservations.* Either registrants will deal directly with the hotel, or you will provide the hotel with a rooming list.

12. *Reservations cutoff date*. The date when the facility returns the room block to the inventory for sale to customers at the over-the-counter rate, usually thirty days prior to the event. This is sometimes negotiable.

13. *Function space requirements*. In addition to outlining how much space will be required, it is a good idea to note the specific meeting rooms on hold. If the size of the meeting may be adjusted, set specific dates for review.

14. *Meeting room rentals*. This may be a flat fee or a sliding scale, based on sleeping room pickup.

15. *Sliding scale rental charges*. Meeting room rental charges are based on the room pickup. If the commitment is met, there may be no charge for room rental. (If you contract for 100 rooms and only pick up 75 rooms, your meeting room rental charge may reflect the reduced number with a higher rental charge.)

16. *Twenty-four-hour hold*. When the meeting rooms are re-served on a full 24-hour basis, they may not be used by the facility, even during downtime.

17. *Setup charges*. Occasionally, a contract appears with room setup charges. Look for this clause to avoid charges for which you are unprepared. Many facilities do not charge for setup; this is a negotiable item.

18. *Reassignment of space*. Specify which meeting rooms are booked. Then room changes may not occur without prior notification from the hotel and written approval from the organizer.

19. *Room deposits*. The specific dates when deposits are due must be noted. Also, be certain you can't lose the reservation because of a missed deposit. Require that the facility notify you of a due date for a deposit.

20. *Billing and handling of the master account*. Who will be assigned to your group account? Who will be permitted to sign on the account? What are the specifics? What charges will be on the account? What charges are individuals responsible for? These must be addressed. In many instances, the meeting will add the room and tax to a master account, but the individual is responsible for all other charges.

21. *Cancellation policy*. In the event of cancellation, the facility will expect compensation for lost anticipated revenue in the areas of sleeping rooms, meeting room rental, and food and beverage functions. There are numerous formulas for cancellation charges; they must be outlined in detail. If the meeting cannot occur as contracted, consider postponement rather than cancellation because it is less expensive. (The facility should also be held liable in the event it cancels the booking. The facility would be responsible for costs incurred from the cancelled booking. These items should be listed and may include airline tickets, marketing costs, rebooking efforts, etc.)

22. *Attrition for food and beverage events*. There will be a penalty if you reduce the stated number of food and beverage events. The attrition clause may require substantial payment for events that are cancelled, taken off-premises, or drastically reduced due to low attendance.

23. *Rate caps*. When the contract is written for a meeting that is two or more years away, it is reasonable to assume that rates may rise by the meeting date. However, there should be a cap on the percentage of the rate increase. This applies to rooms as well as food and beverage. (*Note:* It is also possible that rates may decrease, and this should be addressed in this clause.) (During and for many months after the Gulf War, room rates dropped sharply.)

24. *Renovation and construction*. Require prior notice if renovation and/or construction should be planned during your meeting that will provide you with an option to cancel. Should you opt to run your meeting during renovation, there should be a guarantee that you will not be disturbed.

25. *Quiet enjoyment clause*. This states that the buyers (the group) have the right to rental of the space without disturbance during the time it is being used. This clause is meant to protect the group from undue noise, which may adversely impact the meeting.

26. *Insurance coverage*. Both parties should outline the insurance coverage, and special insurance needs should be noted. Be certain you and the hotel have adequate insurance. Check with the company attorney regarding company policy and off-premises insurance riders.

27. *Union contract renewal*. It should be stated when a union contract is up for renewal. It is risky to run a meeting during the contract renewal period, in case of a strike.

28. *Arbitration clause.* Determine if your company is in favor of arbitration or against it prior to signing a contract that agrees to it. Arbitration is faster and less expensive than litigation; however, binding arbitration eliminates the right to an appeal if the judgment is unfavorable.

29. *AV (audiovisual) company (in-house equipment rental).* It is not unusual for a hotel to provide in-house AV service. For those who prefer to use an outside company, the release from charges for this privilege should be noted in the contract.

30. *Arrival of materials for the package room.* The hotel package room will receive shipments of group meeting materials prior to the program. Package room hours should be noted and hotel policy clearly stated.

31. *Telephone surcharges.* Negotiate away from surcharges. Documentation of the negotiation should be in the contract.

32. *Gratuities.* The policy for gratuities should be clearly stated, and the group should identify plans for tipping. The safest tipping is through the master account on payout slips. You may give your convention services manager the names of those to receive gratuities, along with the amounts on forms (called payout slips) provided by the hotel. The hotel will distribute the gratuities, and the amounts will be charged to your master account.

33. *Governing law.* In the event of a dispute, this clause states where the litigation will take place and which state's laws will apply.

34. *Signage.* Some hotels have rigid regulations regarding signs. If signage is an important part of a large meeting, terms should be negotiated and agreed to.

35. *Exhibit handling.* The loading dock time in and time out of the facility can impact heavily on cost. All requirements and possible limitations should be negotiated and discussed.

36. *Minimum prices for food and beverage functions.* Some hotel contracts will produce a clause stating that there is a minimum amount that must be spent for breakfast, luncheon, or dinner. Negotiate this clause out of the contract. It is unreasonable to be locked into minimums if the meeting does not warrant it.

37. *Safety and fire codes.* The contract should document that the facility meets all required safety and fire codes.

38. *Americans With Disabilities Act (ADA)*. The contract must specifically outline compliance with the ADA regulations.

39. *Termination*. Acts of God or acts by third parties, such as an airline strike or a hotel union strike, permit a party to terminate the contract without penalty. The party terminating the contract has no control over the situation (the act of God), which will interfere with the event.

40. *Hold harmless*. Both parties should agree to hold the other not responsible for negligent occurrences, such as an elevator failure or some other incident that interferes with the meeting.

41. *Occupancy reports*. If not in the contract, periodic occupancy reports are difficult to obtain. Occupancy reports are generated by the reservations department and list all those in your group who have confirmed reservations. This report includes arrival date, departure date, number in party, room type, and special requests.

The items listed are just some of those that may be negotiated and included in a contract. Should there be a dispute, a clearly stated contract, with all parameters defined, is the best form of protection for both parties. Remember to keep a paper trail; document all verbal commitments with a response fax or letter. All print materials and correspondence should be dated and as formal as possible.

Amending a Contract

When contracts need to be amended (whether with minor or significant changes), the following procedures should be followed. If the changes are minor, note them in the margin of the contract, initial and date the changes, and return them for inclusion in and revision of the contract. Be certain to forward the amended document with a cover letter, which outlines the changes and requests that either the changes be countersigned and dated with a return for contract approval *or* the contract be revised per the notations submitted for inclusion.

If the changes are significant, write the amendment as you wish it and send the contract back, with a cover letter requesting changes/

addendum be incorporated into the contract and resubmitted for your approval.

Signing a Contract

While you may not sign the contract, you can assist those in your company who must come to terms with a contractual offer by knowing the current hotel/buyer climate and advising them as to current issues and realistic expectations. A careful review and notation of contractual problem areas will be greatly appreciated and will make for a smoother negotiation process. When in doubt as to procedure, contact your corporate attorney or retain counsel on a consultation basis.

Note that a contract is a binding, legal document. Be cautious about signing a contract. If you are not a corporate officer or an employee with the authority to sign a contract, you will want to consult with an attorney to be certain that, in this instance, you may do so. Independent meeting planners only sign contracts as an agent for the client so as to keep responsibility with the client. You may wish to do the same if required to sign a contract; you may wish to note that you are acting on behalf of your company.

Checklist—Contracts

☐ Review contract with legal counsel.
☐ Ask counsel about signing as an agent (if required to sign the contract).

General Information

☐ Proper identification of your meeting
☐ Specific dates listed in contract
☐ Exact rates to be paid
☐ Number of rooms to be occupied each night
☐ Allowance for early arrivals
☐ Allowance for early departures (short stays)
☐ Cutoff dates (specific dates and times)

- ☐ Guarantees
- ☐ Deposits
- ☐ Check-in and checkout
- ☐ Special rates, such as for staff
- ☐ Number of suites
- ☐ Complimentary room agreement
- ☐ Kind of meeting and meeting room requirements
- ☐ Names of meeting rooms to be used
- ☐ Rental, if any, for meeting room
- ☐ All additional charges in connection with meeting rooms
- ☐ Shipping instructions
- ☐ Package room and storage requirements

Billing Information

- ☐ Setup of master account
- ☐ Person(s) signing
- ☐ Payment arrangements
- ☐ Signature authorizations in your group

Food and Beverage

- ☐ Number of functions
- ☐ Number of attendees at each function (estimate)
- ☐ Prices
- ☐ Guarantees
- ☐ Gratuities, services, and taxes

Services

- ☐ Parking
- ☐ Transportation
- ☐ Activity fees

4

Suppliers and Services

You, as the meeting planner, are the buyer of many services that are critical to the implementation and success of your meeting: hotels or rooming facilities, travel, entertainment, tours, and dining. The suppliers that can provide these services include airline companies, travel agents, destination management companies, and ground and tour operators.

Many suppliers are members of their local Convention and Visitors' Bureau (CVB). Ready access to these services is only a telephone call away.

The Convention and Visitors' Bureau

In addition to assisting with identification of appropriate and available facilities for your meeting, the Convention and Visitors' Bureau will provide you with supplier contacts, registration services, promotional materials (such as postcards, shell brochures, visitor's maps, photographs, and slides), other production items, and postmeeting evaluations.

It is important to note that some CVBs are private and some are public; their structure and services vary. When you contact the CVB in the destination of your choice, be sure to clarify their role and ask if they are private (hotels and restaurants pay a fee to be members) or public (divisions of a chamber of commerce or agency of the government). Also, be sure to ask which of their services are free and which are not.

At the time of your program, a CVB will provide the following:

- Visitors' guides
- Local maps
- Lists of events
- Tour guides
- Shopping and dining brochures (outlining the best in the area)
- Tickets to special events (sometimes discounted, sometimes not)
- Staffing

The guides may be ordered in numbers sufficient for distribution to the meeting attendees; there may be a minimal charge from some CVBs for the materials. CVBs are also a resource for speakers, interpreters, registrars, news releases, appropriate VIP gifts, parking permits, and official greetings.

One additional option would be third-party housing services that will assist with booking rooms and dealing with large meetings. A city-wide meeting with requirements for housing in no less than ten hotels will frequently opt to contract with a third-party housing service instead of a CVB.

Note: CVBs will not recommend one site or vendor over another, nor will they negotiate rates.

Airlines and Group Travel Agencies

Whenever possible, before you lock in meeting dates, you will want to check with air carriers or a group travel agent for date feasibility. Some dates may fall during peak travel periods (such as President's week), and it may not be possible to obtain the needed number of tickets. Even if they are available, the price may exceed your budget.

Airfares are based on peak travel periods, number in the group, and destinations. Inquiries to individual airlines should be directed to those in charge of group and/or meeting and incentive sales.

Airlines and group travel agencies may provide the following:

- Upgrades
- Group fares
- Cargo and shipping assistance

- Special assistance (such as preboarding and lounge privileges)
- Onboard amenities (including free headsets, free drinks, and special films)
- Staff travel
- Arrival/departure manifests
- Advance seat selection
- Promotional assistance (brochures, posters, videos, slides, and shells, which are predesigned pieces used for promotional purposes).

Airlines should provide information about their on-time performance, lost baggage procedures, handling of schedule changes, and frequency of flights. It is important to make the assessment regarding connections and feeder airlines if the meeting attendees will be flying into a destination from many different locations.

As airfares dramatically increased, airlines have become creative and developed zone fare pricing for groups and incentives and are courting the meeting and incentive business.

The major airlines (in alphabetical order) in this playing field are:

- American Airlines First Call Program (with a Web site)
- Continental
- Delta Meeting Network (two Web sites to service the meetings and incentive groups)
- Northwest
- TWA
- United

The carrier of choice, depending on the selection of destination, should be contacted as basic specifications are known. Each airline has a slightly different plan, but all are anxious to work with and for the meetings groups. Check Web sites for possible links.

Many corporations have a travel policy that will guide purchases and systems. For those working through the corporate travel agent of record, it is necessary to coordinate all aspects of travel with the agent.

Airlines and travel agents are aware of current travel trends, prices, problems, changes, and anything positive or negative that may impact on group travel. Use them as a partner and resource for the following three types of information:

1. *Travel patterns.* If you are weighing one destination against another, an airline representative or group travel agent can advise whether one destination is better than the other based on flight patterns, volume, connections, and even traveler preferences.

2. *Blackout periods.* There are specific travel dates when the consumer traffic is so heavy (such as around Thanksgiving or Christmas) that the airlines will not book group travel. In fact, it would be foolish to book travel for a meeting at those times as prices would be at their peak, and it would be difficult to obtain the necessary volume of seats.

3. *Best/worst travel dates.* Just as with blackout periods, there are days during the week that have heavy volume due to corporate/business travel and traffic patterns. This is carefully tracked by the airlines; they will share this information with you.

Destination Management Companies

Destination management companies (DMCs) are experts about their specific destination and surrounding areas. They have established relationships with vendors in their immediate locale and offer a variety of services. DMCs can provide:

- Airport to facility transportation
- Recommendations for theme parties in unusual local venues
- Buying clout
- Specialty spouse programs
- Team-building programs
- Musicians and entertainers for specific events
- Custom programs for individual group needs

How to Select a Destination Management Company

Obtain current references. Ask the sales director in the facility of choice for client lists and the project case histories. Check to see if they are a member of a DMC network or other major industry associations, such as MPI, ASAE, and PCMA. (See list of industry associations in Chapter 2.) The DMC network maintains client/DMC evaluations, standardized contracting, and proposals. Additional references may be obtained from the CVB, local travel agents, and hotel and airline contacts.

Ground Transportation

It has been noted that ground transportation is the first and last opportunity to impress or irritate attendees. It has also been noted that it is incredibly easy for a transfer mishap to occur.

Many resort and upscale properties will provide limousine service for VIPs attending a meeting at their property. This may be a negotiated item. Services may include a facility shuttle (exclusive use for hotel guests only), a shared shuttle (used by several hotels on one run), or an airport shuttle (a specific round-trip tour beginning at the airport).

When selecting a ground transportation (or limousine) company, you must do the following:

- Verify past and current performance.
- Interview rigidly.
- Set standards.
- Review the checklist.
- Monitor the activity closely.

The arrivals and departures list should be as complete as possible with flight numbers, departure times, name of carrier, and all connection information. In addition, there should be a list of the arrivals' home-office contacts, complete with names and telephone numbers, in case of a missed flight or an emergency change of plans. It is also important to keep one of your staff in your home office as the dispatcher. Contact with someone who both knows the schedules and can be reached by all parties makes for a smooth operation.

In addition to providing transfers from airport to facility, many ground operators are also tour operators or part of destination management companies; they will provide transportation to recreational activities as well as tours for your group.

Speakers and Speakers' Bureaus

The importance of selecting the right speaker for the right audience and the right event may seem obvious but can't be stressed enough. The program chair, in accordance with committee recommendations, will generally lead the search for speakers. However, when you are asked to research and recommend keynoters (luncheon, dinner, and/ or celebrity types), first decide what the topic will be. Consider the objective of the meeting and the desired outcome from the speaker's presentation or appearance. After this is determined, obtain assistance and recommendations from the following associations:

- The National Speakers Association (NSA)
- The American Society for Training and Development (ASTD)
- The American Society of Association Executives (ASAE)
- The International Group of Agencies and Bureaus (IGAB)

(See list of associations in Chapter 2.)

Gale's *Encyclopedia of Associations* will once again be a resource for identification of special industry-related associations from which you can draw expert professionals and speakers.

Speaker fees are always negotiable. The bureaus work with each other and sometimes share commissions when one bureau has an exclusive. A good speaker bureau is interested in satisfying the needs of the client; when it is a nonexclusive bureau, it is free to recommend any and all speakers and entertainers.

Provide the speaker with a fee range, an audience and meeting profile, the length of talk (hire time), payment procedures, and any other requirements for the contract.

Ask for references, outline of talk, and possibly a video. Document a cancellation policy, and ask for a contract from the speaker. In the event of cancellation by either party, there may be cancellation compensation.

Music Licensing

Music licensing has been sticky for a number of years because of the control issue. Broadcast Music, Inc. (BMI) is an agency that oversees and protects music copyrights. When music is required for an event—such as an introduction to a meeting, during the reception, or during any function sponsored by the group—you must obtain a license to play the music and pay a $.05-per-registrant fee. Responsibility for any and all music at a meeting is the responsibility of the conference organizer. This includes music played by an exhibitor at a booth in the exhibit hall.

Vendors as Potential Partners

In addition to the partners already noted, there are many other vendors that provide services for meetings and conferences. These include the following:

- Decorating services
- Entertainment/staging and production companies
- Independent meeting professionals and consultants
- Audiovisual companies
- Awards/incentives and premium companies
- Caterers and florists

Industry associations and publications, as well as the sales office of your hotel, are all excellent sources of information for introduction to and selection of vendors.

Checklist—Ground Transportation or Tour Operator

☐ Passenger list
   ☐ Ages
   ☐ Positions

- [ ] VIPs
- [ ] Number in group
- [ ] Grade and style of the hotel/facility
  - [ ] Distance from the airport
  - [ ] Arrival during peak traffic time
  - [ ] Specialists in VIP and LIMO service
  - [ ] Other services
  - [ ] Use for additional events
- [ ] Tours
- [ ] Transfer to off-premises event
- [ ] Insurance in force and adequate
- [ ] Reference from the hotel
- [ ] Reference from the city
- [ ] The arrival
  - [ ] At a major airport
  - [ ] At a small airport
- [ ] Time the company has been in business
- [ ] Company bonded
- [ ] Company insured (obtain verification)
- [ ] Appearance of personnel
- [ ] Turnover of personnel
- [ ] Variety of fleet
- [ ] Size of fleet (for backup)
- [ ] Condition of vehicles
- [ ] Sufficient luggage space
- [ ] Additional vehicle for luggage

Coaches

- [ ] Toilets
- [ ] Microphones
- [ ] Number of vehicles available
- [ ] Passenger capacities
- [ ] Signage

Drivers

- ☐ Length of service
- ☐ Bonded
- ☐ In uniform
- ☐ Language capabilities

Charges

- ☐ Minimum hours
- ☐ Costs and cancellation policy
- ☐ Charges from garage or just for transfer
- ☐ Billing procedure
- ☐ Routing options

Guides

- ☐ Languages
- ☐ Certified
- ☐ Appearance

Checklist—Hiring a Speaker

- ☐ Obtain references.
- ☐ Check credentials and references of the representing speaker bureau.
- ☐ Forward a profile of the meeting attendees to the speaker.
- ☐ Forward the program goals and objectives to the speaker.
- ☐ Outline the expected outcome of the talk (entertaining, training, motivational).
- ☐ Ask to see an outline of the speaker's talk.
- ☐ Ask to see a copy of the contract.
- ☐ Forward a copy of your company contract to the speaker.
- ☐ Outline all parameters in your contract.
- ☐ Determine length of talk.
- ☐ Verify expected arrival and departure time.
- ☐ Specify who will provide transportation and what costs will be assumed (the speaker pays and is reimbursed or arrangements are coordinated by you and made for the speaker).

☐ Determine type of transportation (upper-class, coach).

☐ Provide meet-and-greet service.

☐ Specify the procedure for transportation charges.

☐ Outline who provides the introduction.

☐ Document the procedure for handouts (who provides them, who prints them, how many are needed, when are they needed for reprinting).

☐ Determine audiovisual requirements.

☐ Verify special room setup.

☐ Outline cancellation policy (including penalties and payment policy if the speaker cancels, and cancellation fees if the organization cancels—both based on nearness to the event).

☐ State if there is a possibility of cancellation due to low registration.

☐ Determine if speaker cancels whether he or she will provide a replacement.

☐ Specify that speaker may not provide the same talk for a competitor within a certain number of weeks.

Checklist—Airline Services

☐ Will they provide group fares?

☐ Are fares negotiable?

☐ How many free tickets?

☐ Will they provide upgrades?

☐ Will they pay for site visit?

☐ Will a deposit be required? If so, when?

☐ Will the airline provide videos, slides, brochures, or shells?

☐ Will they help with promotion?

☐ Will they assist with air cargo?

☐ Will they provide luggage tags? Special baggage handling?

☐ Are there free headsets?

☐ Do they supply free drinks?

☐ Does the group warrant lounge privileges?

☐ Are there preboarding privileges?

Checklist—Convention and Visitors' Bureau Services

- ☐ Research of facilities for availability
- ☐ Introduction to facility
- ☐ On-site appointments with appropriate hotel executives
- ☐ List of ground operators (tour operators) and DMCs
- ☐ Knowledge of local taxes, policies, events that may affect meeting (marathons, local festivals)
- ☐ Housing for large meetings
- ☐ Pre- as well as on-site registration services and personnel
- ☐ Secretarial services
- ☐ Translators
- ☐ News releases
- ☐ Official greetings
- ☐ Maps of city for distribution to attendees
- ☐ Restaurant guides
- ☐ Shopping guides and special discounts
- ☐ Discounted tickets for local events
- ☐ VIP gifts
- ☐ Posters and signs
- ☐ Welcome letters/packets

Glossary

agent   A bureau or person who is retained to find engagements for speakers and entertainers.

arrivals   Passengers when they arrive at a terminal.

blackout period   Period when group travel is not booked and rates are at peak.

boarding pass   The seat assignment and airline boarding card ticket.

Broadcast Music, Inc. (BMI)   Protective agency for musical copyrights.

bulkhead   The seats facing the section divider on an aircraft.

business class   An upscale seating section (midrange between coach and first class).

carrier   The airline company that transports passengers.

coach   A term used to describe upgraded bus for group transfers and tours; an inexpensive fare (economy).

Convention and Visitors' Bureau (CVB)   An agency dedicated to promote a destination and service meetings at that city.

departures   Passengers when they are departing on an airline from a terminal.

destination management company   A company designed to service groups in a very specific geographic area.

ground operator   A company transferring passengers and providing tours.

group travel   The meeting attendees' travel to and from a destination.

housing   Company handling the hotel registration for a large meeting at a destination.

in-house   An agency designed as the official agent for a company or association, either on-site or in their own offices.

keynote   The main address to a meeting audience by a speaker considered to be a draw.

overbooked   When an airline sells more seats than are on a plane to allow for the no-show factor.

preboarding   When your group is permitted to board before the other passengers.

shells   Partially preprinted, color promotional material advertising a destination; the balance of copy would promote your meeting.

tour operator   The same as a ground operator but may offer more services (such as tours in addition to transfer from airport to hotel).

travel agent   A licensed person or business group who receives commission for making air or hotel reservations.

upgrades   When a coach ticket holder is moved up to business class or first class.

video   Promotional material on video about the airline and destinations.

vouchers   Tickets or passes that buy drinks and headsets or other amenities on a flight.

zone fares   Fares based on distance from point of departure.

5

Food and Beverage

What kinds of food and beverage events are needed for your meeting? What room set will enhance your events? Planning and negotiating costs, as well as understanding the value of food and beverage service to the facility, are important. The menu and the food and beverage functions are important parts of a meeting. It's a fact: Food makes people feel good.

For the hotel, food and beverage service is a significant revenue producer. For meeting organizers, it is an opportunity to sustain a positive atmosphere or to create one. Food and beverage can drive hordes of people into an area (such as an exhibit hall), the reception is a good networking tool, and some food functions are designed to be group "icebreakers." The goals of the meeting and budget allocations will help you determine what kind of food and beverage events you want at a specific program.

Since food and beverage functions are firmly locked into contracts, it is important to plan food functions prior to signing the contract. Try not to include tentative food and beverage events in your contract. If you commit to an event, you may be responsible for it even if it doesn't take place. On the other hand, if you wait to plan a function, the space you need might not be available for you.

When developing the meeting specifications or RFP (request for proposal), you should estimate the number of events and description of these events as closely as possible. By the time you conduct your site visit, the exact number of attendees may be the only outstanding question. Providing a conservative estimate is prudent. It is permissible to shift the date of the event from one night to another, *but* it is financially risky to cancel an event. If you do, you will pay for it, either by a financial formula constituting attrition or in full, depending on the contract terms.

On the site visit, you will have an opportunity to observe the hotel's or facility's catering operation. If possible, observe another group function on-site. Ask your sales contact to give you a copy of the banquet event order (BEO) for that particular event. If there is a confidentiality issue regarding price, ask for the BEO without the prices included.

Menu Issues

Dated Menu

During your site visit, obtain a complete set of current, dated menus with all available items and prices. This is to ensure that any future price increases will be reasonable (such as 6 percent a year). Perhaps the cost of living index could be a guide. Dated menus serve as documentation of prices at the time the contract is signed, and they provide a baseline from which price increases may be negotiated and agreed to. For example, if a luncheon selection is priced at $25 at the time of the contract agreement, the contract may specify that no more than 6 percent annually may be applied to the price.

Hotels have many different ways of pricing events; a menu review (with pricing) is imperative. For example, if a cocktail party or reception is not a scheduled event in your specs, the hotel sales representative may eliminate the cocktail section listings from your package. However, there are items on the cocktail menu that could be selected for a light supper or even a light buffet luncheon. You want an opportunity to review these options and be able to use them, especially if you have budgetary constraints.

Minimum Pricing

Some contracts require that a minimum amount of money be spent for a particular function and that there be minimum prices for each event. It is better to negotiate these clauses out of your contract.

Tax and Gratuity

When costing the planned menu, it is necessary to calculate the "plus-plus" into the budget. The plus-plus is tax and gratuity, which can add a substantial amount to each food function.

Menu Within a Budget

When selecting a menu while required to adhere to budget considerations, work closely with the catering manager, convention services manager (CSM), food and beverage director, and/or the chef.

Much time has been spent (by the chef and his or her staff) creating menus that are enticing, currently in style (food styles and patterns do change), varied, as cost-effective for the buyer as possible, and profitable for the hotel. Hotels are reluctant to modify the printed menus, but if you give them a budget within which they can work and advise them of your anticipated outcome, more often than not, they will come up with a menu that meets or exceeds your expectations.

The menu should be consistent with the desired goal or meeting objective. There are six considerations when planning a menu:

1. The meeting type and meeting objective
2. Entertainment factors (speakers, music, dancing)
3. Food preferences, creativity, and availability (linked to locale)
4. Room size, group size, and/or event location
5. Type of service and guest profile
6. Amount of time allocated for the function

Food Functions

Food and beverage functions include all of the following:

- Breakfast
- Coffee breaks or intermissions
- Luncheon
- Dinner
- Cocktail receptions
- Brunch

- Theme parties and banquets
- Light late-night suppers
- Receptions
- Box lunches

Breakfast

The range of breakfast options is substantial. One can opt for a full sit-down breakfast, a full buffet breakfast, a more limited but still substantial continental breakfast, or a simple basic coffee service. In the morning, energy is needed to fuel the body for the day. A full breakfast buffet gives all attendees choices. Always include foods rich in carbohydrates (such as bagels) in the morning, along with grains (such as bran, granola, and oatmeal) and fresh fruit. (Fiber keeps blood sugar levels high for long periods, thereby increasing energy.)

Coffee Breaks or Intermissions

The coffee break may or may not offer food along with the coffee. When it is called a "coffee refill" or "refresh," it is more coffee added to the morning breakfast. This is a replenishment of the coffee only during the morning intermission. Afternoon coffee breaks are less often used; it is more popular for an afternoon break to be more creative fare and health breaks. Health breaks may consist of bowls of fresh fruit and yogurt or a dedicated apple break, along with apple cider and fruit drinks (as opposed to soda). Some groups still, however, prefer coffee, cookies, bottled water, and soda.

Luncheon

Anything goes, from light fare (sandwiches and beverage) to a substantial sit-down luncheon. Much depends on the afternoon's planned activity. Usually keep lunch light, with tuna or other fish and salads, including those topped with sliced breast of chicken, bean salads, tabouli, and more fruit. The hotels have produced low-calorie, high-energy luncheons as tastes have changed. They are very willing to work with you.

Cocktail Receptions

The cocktail reception is the largest revenue stream for a facility in the food and beverage area. The trend has shifted from only hard liquor to wine, beer, and bottled water. Though a full bar may be required for a reception, many events provide only wine, beer, soda, and bottled water.

Dinner

A light supper to a substantial sit-down or full buffet dinner may be served. The evening dinners require a little less concern with healthy diet and energy foods as the workday is over and the festivities begin. The cost of large sit-down dinners can be substantial. If budget is a consideration, catering can suggest foods that are in season. Also, the per-person price may be reduced if another group is in-house and you agree to the same menu that they have selected.

Labor carries a high price tag. The less labor that is required, the more reasonable the function; labor in the kitchen translates to additional dollars for a buffet dinner or banquet.

Receptions

These may be the introduction either to a substantial dinner or the event itself. The variety and options are incredible. Some receptions resemble light suppers while others are a precursor to the main event. The objective of the function will drive the menu selection. Keep in mind that labor will have a direct bearing on price: If there is a great deal of labor required to produce the event (hors d'oeuvres that require much preparation), the cost will increase. A carving station, even with the added charge for a carver, may be more cost-effective when you consider the servings per person and the elimination of the back-of-the-house labor.

As with dinners, the evening receptions require little less concern with healthy diet and energy foods because work is finished and the fun is beginning.

Your job is to create menus that provide conferees with healthy, tasty, desirable foods designed to increase their energy during a day of meetings. The chef and banquet director will assist in developing a daily menu that is high in energy.

Locations

Functions may be held anywhere, but the most commonly used areas are ballrooms, private smaller rooms on a property, a patio or garden, a rooftop, a balcony, a suite, and facility restaurants.

Receptions and dinners may also be held at alternative sites, such as in a convention center, conference center, museum, historical building, private club, opera house, botanical garden, yacht, restaurant, or other special events facility.

Prices

Food prices vary widely from region to region. The publications listed as industry resources accumulate data for their readers periodically. If a group is price-sensitive, it would be beneficial to check with the local Convention and Visitors' Bureau and obtain information about current prices at a specific destination.

Since it takes time to develop a good menu, do not put off this important task until the last moment. Plan it well in advance of the deadline, and review the selections with the chef or catering/banquet manager.

The Banquet Event Order

A written, itemized menu should be forwarded to the convention services manager or the banquet manager. Note prices for each item ordered, the anticipated number of people expected for the function, setup requirements, and specific times of the function. The facility will in turn produce a banquet event order and forward it to you for your approval. If there are no changes, the BEO becomes gospel for the service staff. Any changes, additions, or deletions must be made with the approval from the banquet office in a timely fashion.

Guarantees

The required guarantee is the number of people you will pay for even if they are no-shows. The set number will usually be required no less than seventy-two hours prior to the event. This requirement will increase if a weekend intervenes. As a rule, a facility will use the following equation:

- If the guarantee is for 100 dinners, set 5 percent to 10 percent above the guarantee (105 to 110 persons).
- If the guarantee is for 500 dinners, set 4 percent above the guarantee (520 persons).
- If the guarantee is for 1,000 dinners, set 3 percent above the guarantee (1,030 persons).

This is only a guide as the guarantee/set percentage varies from facility to facility and should be discussed at the time the contract is reviewed.

Hotels will generally impose a charge for an event in a private room consisting of less than twenty persons.

Open Seating

One way to offset giving an unrealistic guarantee when the guarantee number is difficult to assess is to ask the hotel to have open seating (to set linens). Open seating will provide for additional tables to be in the banquet or function room, but with only tablecloths on them (set linens). The number of tables set (be it one, two, or three) will not affect the guarantee until all guaranteed and set places are filled. Then, one by one, the tables will be set and opened to accommodate the additional guests. The guests seated at these tables will be counted and added to the original guarantee number for a final count. It should be noted that for large groups, the dinners served to those at these tables may be different from those served to the main or "guaranteed" group.

Service Options

Sit-Down Style

Functions such as breakfast, luncheon, dinners, and banquets are either sit-down events or buffet-style events. There are two services available for sit-down events:

1. *French service.* Servers place the food on the individual diner's plate. This requires a substantial number of servers, slightly larger aisles for the servers to move about comfortably, and enough space between each diner at the table for proper execution.

2. *Plated service.* The food is placed on each plate in the kitchen and then brought into the dining room and set before each diner. Plates must be preheated and the kitchen close to the function room or dining room.

Buffet Style

The buffet style is controversial in the area of cost. Hotels insist it is the more expensive service, on a per-person basis. Generally, for very small groups, it is not cost-effective. However, there is no denying that it is flexible, can rapidly serve large numbers of diners, and requires less waiter/waitress staff. The buffet style setup offers numerous options, which depend on the number to be served and the style of the function.

Carving stations may be very cost-effective as an addition to a buffet-style event. There is a set charge for carvers who man each station, but the charge is reasonable, usually about $100 per carver. Carvers add to the festivity of the occasion as they serve from set stations around the room and provide a variety of options (such as beef, lamb, turkey, salmon, as well as stations for pasta and the flamboyant crepe).

Theme Party Charges

While some facilities have house decorations they are willing to provide at no charge, many will impose a per-person surcharge for a theme party. It is possible to avoid substantial theme party charges in resorts or facilities that have their own weekly theme nights by scheduling your event on the same night as their theme party. The facility may impose a nominal per-person charge, which will be substantially less than the charge to create your own theme party. You may also opt for a separate, private room or area for your group.

Bar Options

There are two bar options:

1. *Hosted bars.* The meeting sponsors or organizers absorb the cost of the reception, and the guests do not pay for the drinks or to attend. This is sometimes called an "open bar."

2. *Cash bar.* Every guest in attendance pays for his or her own drinks. Bartender costs similar to the carving station, and each station will have one or two bartenders. Some facilities will charge for the bartenders; others will not.

Server-to-guest ratios for cocktail receptions are:

- For an average cocktail party, one bartender for every seventy-five guests.
- For a VIP function, one bartender for every sixty guests.
- When attendance exceeds 100 persons, a second station should be set.

Ways to Purchase Liquor

The most cost-effective option for large groups is to purchase by the bottle. For groups under 100, the selection is limited and thereby reduces the cost-effectiveness. However, for a wine/beer reception, it would be cost-effective to purchase by the bottle, allowing two drinks per person, per hour, for consumption. The following are options for purchasing liquor at a reception or event:

- *By the drink.* You will be charged for exactly the number of drinks consumed. This is sometimes called a charge on consumption. One can opt to use tickets (for better control of consumption) or simply estimate costs using the formula of two drinks per person for a one-hour party.

- *By the person.* A per-person price is set for a designated time; there are no limits on the number of drinks consumed during that time, but the number of persons in attendance must be accounted for by door controls or tickets.

- *By the bottle.* Here you have three different options. You may purchase (1) house brands (unknown brands that may carry the facility name and are the least expensive), (2) call brands (brands that are selected by you), and (3) premium brands (known and accepted brands of distinction that are the highest-priced). When purchasing by the bottle, all prices should include mixers and garnishes. (These are the fixings, such as tomato juice, orange juice, appropriate sodas, lemons, cherries, olives, and cocktail onions.)

Wine/Beverage Consumption

There are thirty-two ounces in a quart bottle, and approximately five glasses of wine in a bottle. Consumption of alcohol at a one-hour cocktail party should average two drinks per person. Again, much depends on the group profile and the event.

Trends usually dictate what is ordered. Fifteen years ago, hard liquor (gin, vodka, scotch) were the drinks of choice; then white wine became the most popular drink. Today red wine (such as Merlot) is selected 40 percent of the time. Wine, beer, and bottled water are very well received at receptions, with little call for hard liquor.

Considering that all attendees do not arrive at the moment a reception begins nor do all stay until the end, and that while some drink four glasses of beverage, some will drink none or one, the current average is two drinks per person, per hour.

Electronic Pour/Free Pour

Because liability is an ominous issue, you might want to request that the bartenders at your function use a limiter (electronic pour). A limiter is a control mechanism on the top of the bottle that limits the pour to one ounce. The other option is a free pour, which allows the bartender to freely pour from the bottle. This generally amounts to more than an ounce of liquor and more money.

Liquor Liability

Because of the high liability with hosted events, it is imperative that the planner enforce corporate rules and that the facility is made aware of these policies. To keep the liability issue in perspective, consider that in more than forty states, there is a "dram shop law." The dram shop law extends liability, in the event of an incident due to excessive alcohol consumption, to the social hosts of a cocktail reception.

Assign a staff person to monitor liquor consumption and to alert you immediately in case of a problem. Hotels and facilities are aware of the liquor liability and will work with you to ensure the smooth handling of any problems that may arise.

There are eight ways to reduce liquor liability:

1. Require a one-ounce pour, not a free pour.
2. Limit the length of service; do not extend the reception beyond the designated time.
3. Use professional bartenders only; they know how to handle problems.
4. Avoid self-service—no kegs of beer (even for theme parties, unless there is a server).
5. Provide an abundance of nonalcoholic beverages.
6. Provide food.
7. Have someone monitor the reception.
8. Provide transportation or a sleeping room when necessary.

Room Setup

Rounds are tables that measure sixty inches in diameter or seventy-two inches in diameter and are generally set for luncheon or dinner. The number of guests who may be seated at these tables is eight to ten at the 60-inch round; the 72-inch round may seat up to twelve guests. There should be a minimum of two feet for aisle space.

There are numerous buffet-style setups—from serpentine (curved tables put together in an "S" design) to a double layer or tier on the tables. These will generally be set by the facility in the best possible way for each function. To eliminate guests waiting in long lines, there should be either several tables and an arrangement that permits a line on each side of the tables or several serving stations, as the room space and group size will permit.

Timing/Coordination

Coordination between the planner and the facility will provide opportunity for successful adjustments. The BEO is only as good as the last change or modification. If the morning program is not on schedule and it appears the luncheon will be off-schedule (either early or late), the CSM must be notified so the kitchen (back of the house) can adjust to the revised schedule.

In the case of the late-breaking session, the kitchen can then preset a salad or first course. Much depends on the menu, of course. For a program that will break early, the kitchen staff needs to jump into high gear and make whatever adjustments they can. They will do it, but they do, however, need your cooperation and timely communication.

Checklist—Food and Beverage

☐ Solidify room assignment for each event.
☐ Obtain dated menus.
☐ Establish food and beverage budget (include plus/plus).
☐ Establish timelines for menu planning.
☐ Meet the chef.
☐ Meet the banquet manager or catering director.
☐ Provide the convention services manager with printed program.
☐ Discuss event style and options
    ☐ Buffet
    ☐ Reception
    ☐ Sit-down event
    ☐ Formal
    ☐ Informal
    ☐ Room setup
    ☐ Service style
    ☐ Service and staff requirements (number per service)
    ☐ Free pour for receptions vs. limited pour
☐ For cocktail receptions select type of service
    ☐ Butler-passed foods
    ☐ Buffet-style service
    ☐ Number of bar setups and bartenders
☐ Liquor charges
    ☐ By the person
    ☐ By the drink
    ☐ By the bottle
    ☐ Cash bar
    ☐ Hosted bar
    ☐ Number of servers per person

- ☐ Determine decorations and if there is a theme
    - ☐ Outside decorator
    - ☐ Facility support
    - ☐ Flowers
    - ☐ Candles
    - ☐ Music
    - ☐ Photographer
- ☐ Other considerations
    - ☐ Liquor laws
    - ☐ Checkrooms
    - ☐ Timing
    - ☐ Microphones
    - ☐ Staging
    - ☐ Table cards
    - ☐ Printed menus
    - ☐ Program
    - ☐ Gifts
    - ☐ Head table
    - ☐ Reserved tables

Glossary

a la carte   Items on the menu that are individually charged as opposed to a set price for an entire meal.

banquet   A formal dinner or gathering.

banquet event order (BEO)   The complete detailed outline of a function or functions, noting item, price, quantity, and serving time.

box lunch   Lunch in a box, usually taken off-premises.

buffet   Self-service; various foods are set on tables in a number of configurations.

by the bottle   Liquor charged for by the full bottle.

by the drink   Liquor charged for by the number of drinks consumed.

by the piece   Food purchased by the piece.

call brands   Brands of liquor selected by the client.

captain   Person in charge of banquet service at food and beverage functions.

cash bar   Guests pay for the drinks.

chef's choice The chef selects accompanying foods to be served with the entree.

coffee break Coffee served during a meeting intermission.

continental breakfast A light breakfast of breads, buns, coffee, and juice.

corkage The charge imposed on alcoholic beverages that are brought into a facility for consumption.

covers The actual number of meals served at a function.

dry snack Minimal food service for receptions, usually pretzels, nuts, potato chips.

electronic pour A mechanism for limiting exact amounts of liquor poured for a drink.

entree The main course.

free pour When the server pours alcohol from a bottle without a limiter.

French service When the server (waiter) serves each item of food directly from the platter to the plate of the individual.

garnish Food decoration.

guarantee The number of meals to be paid for, whether or not they are consumed.

head count The actual number of people at an event.

hospitality suite A suite used to entertain guests.

house brands Lower-priced liquor with an unknown label used by the facility.

maitre d' The head waiter at a function.

minimum The least amount that may be charged, based on numbers of guests.

open bar Bar setup for drinks to be paid by the sponsor.

plated buffet A variety of food set out on tables. It is not self-service; a waiter serves the guests.

plus-plus Tax and gratuities that are added to a price.

premium brands The most expensive brands of liquor.

preset Placement of food prior to seating.

reception A social function with beverage and food.

service charge Charge for the waiters, housemen, and other personnel.

supper A light evening meal.

theme party A festive event with one theme for decorations, food, and entertainment.

union call When union waiters are summoned to serve at a function.

water stations Pitchers of water and glasses set in a specific area for self-service.

yield The number of pieces or portions from any given unit.

6

Exhibits

Many conferences provide tabletop displays that enhance the value of a meeting by providing additional resources and information for the attendees. These displays may be modest table layouts or more extensive booth arrangements. Exhibits are an integral part of a convention or meeting. The basic guidelines in this chapter will assist those who organize meetings, conferences, and conventions with accompanying tabletops and booths.

The Purpose

Exhibits provide an opportunity for attendees to obtain industry-specific information that is relevant to the conference topic or theme. The environment is upbeat; the atmosphere is comfortable and friendly. This is time dedicated to product introduction, information exchange, prospecting, sales, and networking.

Tabletop Displays

Tabletop exhibit areas are a popular exhibit arrangement. Tabletops may be modest in size and inexpensive, yet they offer a variety of options. Exhibits such as these may be placed in the same area as the conference, in the foyer, near the registration area, in a room adjacent to the conference, or in a room on another floor.

When space permits, tabletop display areas may be the location of choice for coffee breaks, program intermissions, and buffet luncheons.

The number of such exhibits can easily approach 60 to 75 tabletops for a meeting of 50 to 1,000 persons. The tables (generally 6 feet by

32 inches or 8 feet by 32 inches) are draped (covered and skirted by the facility) and set in a designated space (10 feet by 10 feet). (See Figure 6-1.)

The tabletop exhibit area will accommodate everything from the display of literature to roll-in equipment for demonstration purposes. Roll-in equipment, such as a computer system or an ultrasound scanner for medical diagnosis, is small and light enough to be transported by the exhibitor. In many instances, it is demonstration equipment (made portable by a stand on wheels). Many hotels do not permit such equipment to enter through their lobby or public areas; they require the portable equipment to enter through the loading dock or other passages designated for freight.

Tabletop exhibitors may provide their own tabletop signage and/or display boards. Display boards or pop-up tabletops are display materials that are brought from conference to conference in a tube or carrying case. These displays unfold into an advertisement/display, which may be set on top of a table. At the end of the meeting, they are unfolded or disassembled, returned to their compact carrying cases, and either shipped or carried to the next meeting.

Tabletop exhibitors may also elect to display banners with their company name, which drape over the front of the tables for identifica-

Figure 6-1. Tabletop exhibits.

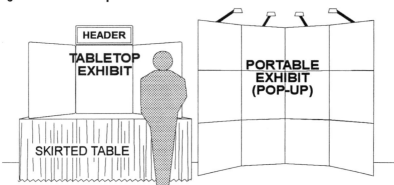

tion/promotion. In some instances, conference organizers may provide standard signage for everyone, in addition to the individual materials.

The rules and guidelines for tabletop displays are first set by the facility (the hotel or conference center) and then by the conference organizers. If a tabletop becomes too similar to a formal booth setup (sits on the floor instead of on a table or extends too high—over 6 feet), the hotel may impose per-table charges.

While many facilities do not charge for the table setup, it is possible there will be charges for rental of the space; you may also be charged anywhere from $50 to $200 for the setup of each table.

The maximum height, width, and overall parameters must be indicated by the planner in written guidelines to the exhibitor. The facility will provide the following guidelines for shipping and receiving of material:

- How the materials should be addressed
- What the target arrival dates are
- Where the materials should be shipped (specific loading dock or other designated area)
- What the parameters for storage of those materials are
- When and how they may be retrieved

Setup times are determined by the organizer, and the space is contracted for directly with the facility. Setup may be scheduled for the night before the conference or the morning of the conference. Strike or dismantle hours are also provided to the exhibitors.

Formal Exhibits

A second exhibit arrangement is the exhibit area or exhibit hall, with draped booths or demarcated areas for each exhibitor. Space allotment is generally 8 feet by 10 feet, 10 feet by 10 feet, or 8 feet by 10 feet. Aisle sizes (10 feet or 12 feet) are guided by facility rules, number of attendees, traffic flow, and fire and safety regulations. (See Figure 6-2.)

Figure 6-2. Exhibit area booth.

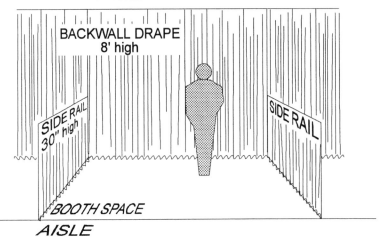

Booth space is sold to exhibitors by the square foot. You will work with a professional exposition company that will provide design options of the exhibit hall for your approval. The design should take into consideration fire and safety requirements, the number of anticipated booths, food services areas (if any), and requirements of the meeting. (See Figure 6-3.)

In addition to the standard booth, the option for additional booths or additional designated space can be offered to potential exhibitors. Sale of two or more booths (peninsula booth) or islands generates additional revenue for the conference sponsors and adds a great deal of variety to the exhibit floor.

Based on the drawing from the contractor or convention services department, the planner will determine how may booths and what type of booths can be offered for sale (see Figure 6-4). There are several booth options:

- *In-line booth.* An exhibit booth or designated space that is in line with all the other booths.
- *Corner booth.* An exhibit booth or designated space with aisles on two sides.

Figure 6-3.   Sample exhibit hall design.

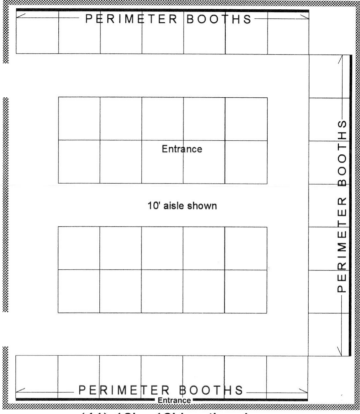

(41) 10' x 10' booths shown

- *Island booth.* Four (or more) exhibit booths or designated spaces with aisles on all sides.
- *Peninsula booth.* Two (or more) exhibit booths or designated spaces that are back to back, with an aisle on three sides.
- *Perimeter booth.* An exhibit booth located on the outside wall(s).

The exhibit area or exhibit hall will usually be in an adjacent ballroom or area near the conference. It should be noted that some professional meetings have guidelines for placement of the exhibit hall as it relates to commercialism at an educational meeting. Medical

Figure 6-4. Exhibit booth options.

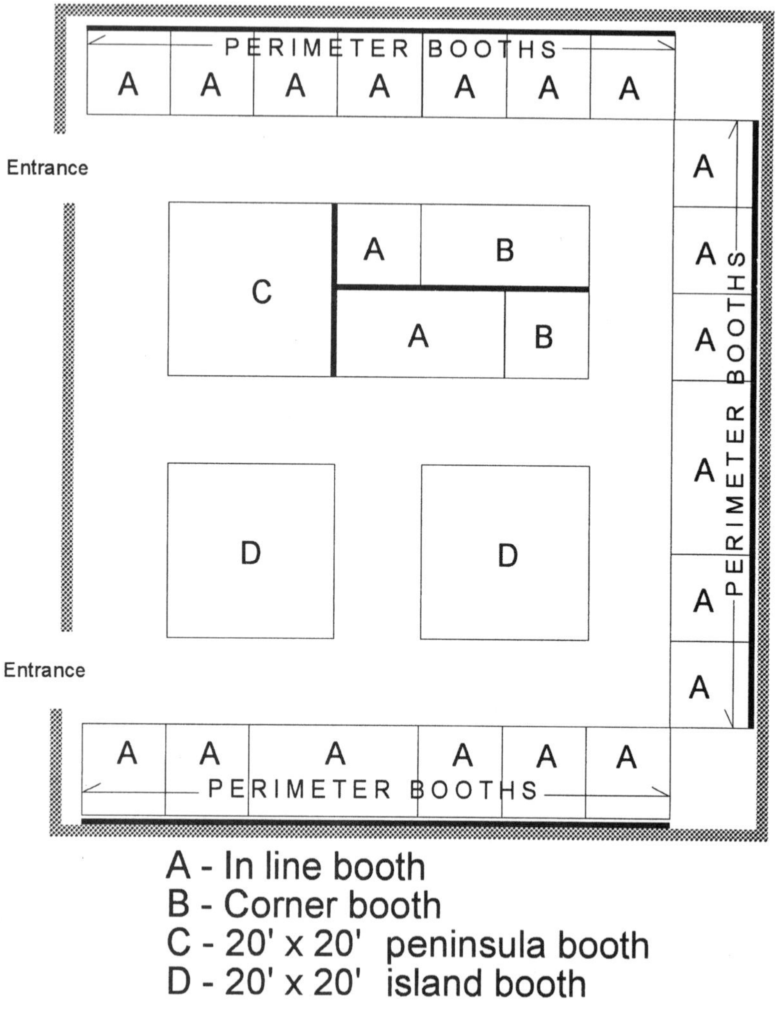

A - In line booth
B - Corner booth
C - 20' x 20' peninsula booth
D - 20' x 20' island booth

associations, for example, follow specific mandates for placement of commercial exhibits at continuing medical education conferences.

Scale Drawings

To return from a hotel or conference center site inspection with scale drawings has more than a small measure of significance for the exhibit floor designer. In an exhibit hall, it is not just the issue of gross square feet versus net square feet, but the interference of sizable poles or support structures throughout the floor, which limit the number of booths.

Budgeting

The fee for exhibiting is generally based on the number of square feet used. For example, a 10 foot by 10 foot booth equals 100 square feet; at $10 per square foot, the exhibitor would pay a fee of $1,000 for the space. Additional charges may be imposed by the show organizers and noted in the marketing and sales agreements/contracts.

Cost factors include the following:

- Rental charged to the conference organizers (on a per-square-foot basis or by flat fee for an exhibit room)
- Expenses incurred to retain the expo company (which may be passed on to the exhibitor or factored into the price per square foot)
- Signage
- Security
- Electrical contracting
- Food and beverage
- Staffing

The show organizers must also pay rental during pre- and postconference periods, which are allocated for setup and teardown of exhibits. Overtime charges for evening setup or weekend hires also have an impact on the budget.

Setup and Dismantle Period

Anywhere from one additional day to two or more days on each side of the conference dates, depending on the magnitude of the show and the complexity of the exhibits, will be needed to set up and dismantle.

Special contractors are retained to assist with carpentry, rental of booth items, assembly of booths, and shipping. A show management office is set up on-site by the exposition company; it is staffed during setup and dismantle periods to troubleshoot and provide whatever assistance is needed.

Food and Beverage

In many exhibit halls, space is also allocated for food and beverage service. If setup is in a dedicated exhibit hall connected to a hotel but operated independently of that hotel, there may be restrictions regarding catering. You may not be able to use a caterer of your choice but may be required to use a designated contractor for the facility. If the exhibit hall is a ballroom in a hotel, the food and beverage may be selected from the general hotel menu.

Prospectus

A prospectus or exhibitor information manual/kit is provided for each exhibitor. The manual contains an application and/or contract, show floor diagram noting booth numbers and space assignments, and a list of all the services available from the exposition or decorating company. These services include but are not limited to furnishings (tables, chairs, decorative plants, stands, waste bins), sign, electrical, telephone, and computers.

Rules and regulations of the specific exhibit are also clearly outlined and defined. These address many important issues:

- Booth height limitations
- Requirements for liability and insurance
- Damage to property
- Fire, safety, and health regulations
- Use of alcoholic beverages
- Floor load
- Subleasing
- Space restrictions

Checklist—Exhibits

☐ Scale drawing floor plans
☐ Dimensions of area
☐ Ceiling heights

☐ Loading dock
    ☐ Size of dock
    ☐ Procedures for receipt of materials
    ☐ Hours of dock operation
    ☐ Access from dock to meeting room or exhibit area
☐ Floor load
☐ Rates
    ☐ Charges—covered
    ☐ Charges—additional
    ☐ Storage rates
    ☐ Rates for removal of materials from storage
    ☐ Weekend charges for receipt of materials
    ☐ Evening charges for receipt of materials
    ☐ Electrician availability and rates
☐ Facility type
    ☐ Hotel
    ☐ Conference center
    ☐ Convention center
☐ Exhibit type
    ☐ Tabletop
    ☐ Full booth setup
☐ Exhibit hours
☐ Exhibit drawings
☐ Coordinate with subcontractor
☐ Insurance requirements
☐ Food and beverage in exhibit area
    ☐ Hours of service
    ☐ Type of service
☐ Fire regulation codes
☐ Security

Glossary

aisle carpet   Carpet installed in exhibit area aisles.
attendance   Number of people at an exhibit.
AV contractor   Supplier of audiovisual equipment.

booth   A set of pipe and drape or hardwall materials in a set number of feet or demarcated area in the exhibit hall.

booth number   The number that identifies the space.

carpenter   On-site to build or install displays.

corner booth   Exhibit space with aisles on two sides.

covered   Tables requiring cloth coverings (registration tables or display tables).

decorating   Dressing the exhibit with carpet, drapes, plants, and flowers.

decorator   The general contractor or exposition company.

dismantle   Take down (strike) the exhibits.

dispatcher   Person responsible for schedule of freight and labor.

draping   Decorating with drapes.

drayage   Transfer of exhibit materials from point of arrival to the exhibit site.

exclusive contractor   The contractor retained to provide services.

exhibit directory   Directory of exhibitors and their location for benefit of the attendees.

exhibit prospectus   Promotional materials sent to "sell" participation in the show.

floor load   The maximum amount of weight per square foot that a floor can support.

floor manager   The person retained to supervise the exhibit area.

four-hour call   A minimum work period for union labor.

freight forwarder   A shipping company.

gross square feet   The total amount of space in an exhibit hall (does not account for space that is unusable).

island booth   Four or more exhibit spaces with aisles on all four sides.

loading dock   The area designated for receipt of goods via truck or other shipping.

move-in   Date set to begin installation.

move-out   Date set to begin dismantling.

net square feet   The amount of usable space available for exhibits; takes into account space not usable, such as poles and support mechanisms.

peninsula booth   Two or more exhibit spaces, back to back, with an aisle on three sides.

pipe and drape   Metal tubing supporting drapes, which form booths and separate exhibit booths.

pop-ups   Display materials used at exhibits that are housed in compact carrying cases for ease of transport.

quad box   Four electrical outlets in one box.

service kit   A packet of information and order forms for the exhibitors.

show manager   The person responsible for all aspects of the exhibit.

show office   The management office at the exhibit.

side rail   The low divider wall (usually on the sides of the booths) in the exhibit hall.

skirting   Decorative covering (usually pleated or shirred) around tables, risers, and stands.

space assignment   Booth space assigned to the companies that exhibit.

space rate   Cost per square foot to exhibit.

staging area   The area adjacent to the main event for setup, storage, and dismantling.

strike   Dismantle exhibits.

tabletop display   Portable displays that can be set up on top of a table.

tear down   Dismantle.

7

Special Events

Meetings usually have one or more special events or activities for their attendees. A special event may be any event or function other than the basic educational meeting sessions. Special events may include spouse and family programs (which occur while the attendee is in session) or events held aside from the general educational sessions (which may or may not include the attendee).

Special events include but are in no way limited to the following:

- Golf or tennis tournaments
- Tours
- On- or off-premises dinners
- Cruises
- Theater
- Opera
- Ballet
- Fun runs
- Fishing outings
- White-water rafting
- Hayrides
- Beach parties
- Concerts
- Banquets
- Dinner and dancing
- Costume balls
- Any and all theme parties

Day trips to facilities closed to the general public may sometimes be arranged by the Convention and Visitors' Bureau, the National Tourist Board, or a destination management company. Popular tours include art colonies, historic sites, mansions, and even catered dinners in the private home of a celebrity.

Attendee Profile

Scheduling the event for a group requires review of the attendee profile. Is the audience the same as last year, or are they new attendees for whom you can repeat a previous, successful event? If the group is the same one, the event doesn't have to be bigger or better than last year, but it does have to be different.

Whatever the event, the issue of appropriateness of that event for the meeting attendees must be addressed. A meeting of scientists divulging their findings about a serious illness may need an event in the evening to relieve the pressures of the day; however, it would be highly inappropriate to hire a comedian to lighten the mood at the luncheon.

If the meeting is held in a major city with built-in attractions (such as a concert hall, opera house, or theater), an audience from out of town will generally be receptive to an evening of local entertainment.

For other event options ranging from cruises to art or historical museums, it is advisable to consult with the facility, which may have a list of previously booked special events.

The Corporate Environment

Corporations have numerous occasions for special events. These include:

- Birthdays of high-ranking executives
- Visits from VIPs (either an official corporate visit or a family vacation)
- Media visits (whether to cover a groundbreaking event or to search for a story)
- Board meetings
- Holiday parties

For these special events, refer to your corporate policy manual for specifications regarding ceremonies, gifts, birthdays, retirements, and/ or handling of the press. The protocols should advise a range of ranks for invitation purposes as well as for seating arrangements. (If you have no access to established corporate protocols, you should consult with your administration and research protocols in some of the many books available in major bookstores regarding business protocol and etiquette.) Develop a list of suppliers that can provide engraved items and other high-quality gifts appropriate for VIPs and dignitaries.

You should also maintain a VIP file indicating individual VIP preferences for entertainment and dining. In the case of international VIPs, protocol issues must be carefully addressed and noted as well. These include proper forms of address, proper flag placement, and recognition of dining customs (what food to serve and proper seating arrangements). An excellent source for international protocols would be the United Nations bookstore.

Golf Tournaments

Resort facilities, conference centers, and meeting properties offering outstanding golf are always in demand. Each year, various awards are bestowed on the top-ranked properties; these are heavily promoted in numerous publications and certainly by the facilities themselves. Golf meeting resorts can be researched on the Internet or by calling any of the meeting industry publications listed in the Resources at the end of this book. The best golf courses are ranked by quality and course difficulty, their professional golf staff, the natural beauty of the course, and the hospitality and service of the meeting facility.

If you need to plan a tournament for your meeting, discuss it with your contact at the facility prior to the site visit. If you are not a golfer, be sure to hire the facility golf pro or other golf professional to help you plan the event. Reserve the golf pro's time and the course and coordinate the event before signing a contract with the facility.

For the nonaficionado, the nonplaying spouses, and/or the children, there are other options, such as "Beat the Pro" and putting green obstacle courses. The golf pro will arrange for games that allow non-golfers to work and play with him. In the "Beat the Pro" test, he will allow players to challenge him for prizes. Everyone can play and enjoy the challenge.

New facilities give testimony to the allure of golf and all-encompassing entertainment on one resort property. There are even golf cruises—there is no golf on the cruise ship (perhaps putting?), but the cruise allows for stops at major golf courses.

Golf Incentives

Golf incentives are in great demand. As more and more corporations reward their top-performing sales force or executives, they rely on the popularity of golf and award their employees with several days at an all-expense-paid golf facility.

It cannot be emphasized enough that golf programs require the assistance of a pro. In addition to obtaining handicap information (ranking the players) and scheduling the players, there are awards and gifts that are usually distributed during an incentive.

It is not unusual for substantial rewards to be bestowed on the recipients of an incentive trip. They are company achievers; the rewards, in addition to the trip, may be cash awards or watches. But for a golf incentive, the more likely rewards may include sets of signed golf memorabilia, such as clubs, shirts, and jackets. It would be necessary to be a golfer to know which of these would be most valued. These gifts are distributed during the incentive trip, sometimes quietly, sometimes during an awards ceremony.

Golf incentive locations may be upscale, top-rated golf facilities, such as Doral and Pebble Beach Golf Club in Monterey Peninsula, or they may be scheduled abroad in such dedicated golf destinations as the Algarve in Portugal or Gleneagles, Turnberry, and St. Andrews in Scotland. An opportunity to play the world's most famous courses is a powerful motivator. Incentive budgets may be on the high side and are even higher when famous sports stars are added as an enhancement to the incentive trip. Corporations indicate that the incentives are well worth the cost. There are specialty incentive houses available for varying degrees of assistance. See the Resources at the end of this book.

Tennis Tournaments

Tennis tournaments must be planned for and included in the preliminary specifications. When on the site inspection tour, note the following:

- Number of courts on the property
- Availability of courts for group use
- Allocation of courts for other groups and hotel guests
- Reservation availability during prime time for the meeting attendees

- Cost for reserved courts
- Availability of a tennis pro on-site, his or her services and fees

Some groups will want to bring their own pro (someone who is famous in the particular sport as an added attraction); in this instance, the group organizer may need to obtain permission in case of a right-to-work regulation. Some destinations do not allow the hire of off-premises or nonresident professionals without a permit. (Bermuda is such a destination.)

Family Events

Record numbers of meetings are catering to families, and more specifically, to the children of attendees. Lack of family time is expanding this trend, as are the success stories from those who provide innovative programs for families and children. Kids' and family programs do not deter participation; they drive it.

The inclusion of children and families in such functions as the opening event, meals, or any other special event is becoming very popular. Individual or separate events for the children should also be considered. Meeting sites reflect this trend as the destinations, such as the Orlando Disney properties, with built-in activities for kids are currently the most sought-after. The Baltimore Aquarium, which has an auditorium meeting professional standards on its property, is an example of another good kid site. While the professional parent attends a meeting, the children can enjoy the aquarium. After the meeting and the day at the aquarium, families can come together in another area for dinner and even entertainment.

Dedicated family beach resorts are also popular for families as they provide numerous family sports and activities, such as tennis, golf, fishing, and sailing for all ages.

To offset the issue of liability, subcontract to professionals whose business it is to provide kids' programs. Be certain to obtain current references; verify their track record, their risk management policy, their insurance coverage, and their standards.

What they provide depends largely on the age of the children. From an on-site nursery or playschool to planned activities for older children, a safe setting, proper documentation, and protection against liability are all necessities.

Kids will be kids! Expect the unexpected! These phrases have already become commonplace when discussing the development of kids' programs. Because this audience is young, it is important that all protective methods be used. The planner or subcontractor must provide disclaimers, have parents sign release and consent forms, and maintain sufficient insurance coverage. It would be prudent and cost-effective to have the corporate attorney or industry attorney review all contracts.

Professional Help

Creative and talented, the special events companies produce everything from weddings to inaugural balls. Large production companies are generally the vendor of choice for corporations as they develop huge mega-events, worldwide product introductions, rollouts, and industry trade shows.

Special events professionals create themes, build sets, provide rainbows, and make it rain on cue. Many have solid theatrical or entertainment background with unbelievable technological skill and creativity. Special events enhance meetings, and frequently a serious, difficult message may be delivered to an audience under the protective shield of entertainment for a warmer reception.

If a meeting requires the talents and services of dedicated special events personnel, they can be found through specialty associations such as the Convention and Visitors' Bureau and destination management companies and/or special events companies that are members of the International Special Events Society (ISES). (See Resources at the end of the book for events.)

For lesser productions than extravaganzas or for smaller meetings, an alternative is to retain the services of a destination management company (cultural and event experts in their own geographic area). The DMC (destination management company) can also establish and staff a leisure desk at the facility for the exclusive use of attendees. They are available for consultation, or they can develop the event(s) for your group.

In addition, many resorts have a professional conference department that can offer assistance and make recommendations from a menu of events that are suitable for the attendees, spouses, and/or the entire family.

Resorts may also be an event paradise, with a variety of built-in options such as golf, tennis, and water sports; other offerings that are popular in certain destinations are hot-air ballooning and horseback riding.

Supplier Services

If you need to hire musicians or photographers, or if you are looking for new ideas for kids' and family events, you can rely on the local Convention and Visitors' Bureau, your destination management company, and the recommendations from your facility sales personnel.

To be sure you are on the right track, evaluate your group. Each group has its own personality; one of your major responsibilities is to match the group profile with selected events and activities. For offbeat activities, it is best to try them yourself or obtain a recommendation from a group that has had recent experience with the activity. Remember, however, your opinion is critical because you know your group.

Checklist—Options for Resort Activities

- ☐ Cruises
- ☐ Tours
- ☐ Local sports events
- ☐ Ski locales

- ☐ Water sports
  - ☐ Sailing
  - ☐ Scuba diving
  - ☐ Fishing
  - ☐ Cruises
  - ☐ White-water rafting
- ☐ Hiking/backpacking
- ☐ Horseback riding
- ☐ Tournaments
  - ☐ Golf
  - ☐ Tennis
  - ☐ Marathon
- ☐ Olympics
- ☐ Bike racing
- ☐ Other sports competition
- ☐ An opening
- ☐ Product launch
- ☐ Award ceremony
- ☐ Anniversary
- ☐ Annual meeting
- ☐ Fund-raisers
- ☐ Vendors or partners needed for events
  - ☐ Entertainment (entertainers, musicians, speakers, etc.)
- ☐ Hire/collaborate with
  - ☐ Destination management company
  - ☐ Production company
  - ☐ Convention and Visitors' Bureau
  - ☐ Facility convention personnel—for theme event
- ☐ Professional sports
  - ☐ Tennis
  - ☐ Golf
  - ☐ Water (including boating)

8

Budgeting

by Ronald J. Naples

Budgeting and setting financial goals are often confused as the same activity. They are not. Before a budget can be established, the financial goals for a program must be decided. This is no different from deciding a program's goals and objectives before deciding on the type of program and where it may be held.

Setting Financial Goals

Financial goals must fit into the overall company and program objectives. In some instances, the program objective may be a goodwill goal rather than a profit goal. It might be a year-end celebration designed to build goodwill among the employees and to thank them for a record-breaking year. This program is most likely to be fully funded by a department, with no expectation of making a profit or even of underspending the budget.

Other programs have hard-core financial goals and expect the program to generate a profit. Seminars and training development programs sold to the general public (sometimes with public exhibitions) must produce a profit. The projected profit is determined by at least three factors:

1. *History.* This is how well the program did last year.
2. *Operating funds.* This may be the annual event that produces the majority of the annual budget.
3. *Profit expectation.* The budget may have an expectation of a percentage of profit for the amount of funds invested.

Return on Investment

Whether a program has a goodwill goal or a profit goal, the goal is called a return on investment (ROI), or value of the program. A simple way to assess ROI is to divide net profit by total cost of the program; the result is the percentage of financial profit.

When goodwill is the ROI you seek, you must use alternate measurement tools. This may be the gleam in the eye of the executive host, all attendees leaving with stacks of business cards, or simply the opportunity to celebrate and have a truly good time.

ROI must have meaning to you and your company. It must be measurable, and it must be decided in advance of the program as a financial goal, even though, in some situations, it may not be financial at all.

In order to assess the financial success of a program, you must establish a budget that is designed to accomplish the financial goals you have set. A budget may be as simple as a few figures or a listing of hundreds of accounts in your electronic spreadsheet. Whichever you prefer, use something.

Creating a Budget

A budget is a tool designed to assist you in achieving your financial goals. Think of a budget as a road map that will get you to the goals you seek. But to get there, you must follow a certain path and keep your information current.

Historical Data

Development of a new budget for an existing program requires a review of past performance. How did the program do last year? Were financial goals achieved? The previous budget, along with new quotes for large expense items and adjustment of expenses and revenue to account for inflation, will provide a fairly accurate budget from which to work.

If the program has no history, more research for preparation of the budget is needed. Pursue expense item quotes; make some educated guesses on the revenues based on programs you know your audience attends. Price them within the range you believe they are willing to pay.

A new program may see many changes in its first year; it is important to document the changes and trends as you identify them. This will make planning for the next budget much easier.

Administrative Overhead

In many companies, a specific program budget is part of a department budget that reports into a division budget, which goes into the main company budget. Wherever your funding source, it is important to establish a program budget so you can accurately track expenses. You may be responsible for many program budgets that report into your department budget. In such cases, there are some shared expenses, such as administrative support; this support may be the copier, telephone, messenger service, computer, etc. Collectively these items, along with salaries and benefits, are called administrative overhead. Though they are paid by a department budget, you should list a percentage of the total costs as an expense in each program budget.

Every budget has two items: revenues and expenses. These are spread across line items, or accounts.

Revenues

Revenues take money into the budget and give it spending power. Without revenue to offset expenses, you will forever be in debt. Even with zero-based budgeting, where your goal is not to make a profit but to spend all the revenue taken in, the goal is not to lose money and fall into a negative situation. Revenues can come from these sources:

- Company contributions
- The budget
- Registration fees
- Sale of books, hats, buttons
- Sponsorship
- Franchise fees

Opportunities for revenue are limitless as long as your goals for the program give you such a range. Sometimes program goals are limiting, and the revenue source is simply a company contribution. This is most often the case when the ROI is a goodwill goal.

Fixed Expenses

Expenses to a budget fall into two categories: fixed and variable. Fixed expenses are not adjusted (based on program attendance) and often cannot be changed even if the revenue falls short of expectations. A fixed expense may be the program marketing cost. For example, printing and mailing of brochures occurs well in advance of the program. Certain vendor expenses are also fixed; whether 100 or 150 people attend your function, the fee for an orchestra remains the same.

Contract negotiations for any facet of your program must take into consideration the expense budget you have created. When finalizing contracts, ask yourself how much room you have left for variables in attendance due to weather and other influencing factors. Make sure any agreed-upon deposits or cancellation fees are fees your budget will be able to fund if and when they are needed.

Variable Expenses

Variable expenses can fluctuate based on attendance or other factors. Food and beverage costs are variable expenses; the actual cost varies, based on the number of people guaranteed and in attendance. If a meal costs $50 per person and attendance was estimated at 150 people, the cost would be $7,500. But if the numbers are down and, 48 hours in advance of the event, you guarantee 100 persons will attend, your total cost is only $5,000. This is a variable expense.

Line Items

The line items identify each item the budget accounts for. Each line item will have a name, such as registration fees, breakfast, or room rental. Each line item also has a revenue and expense column. Companies with electronic accounting usually assign a code number to each line item. This permits reports (by code numbers) that show each expense paid in that line, and when it was paid, as well as how much money is left to spend in that line.

Budgets are usually divided into months and can be laid out either manually on budget paper, with lines, rows, and columns, or electronically on computer, using one of the many budgeting and accounting programs that exist. Budgets kept on computer tend to be more current and accurate and, therefore, a better tool for achievement of the program's financial goals.

Using a Budget

Once a quality budget has been put in place, it will serve as your guide through the program planning process. It is the road map that will get you to your destination, which, in the case of your program, is the ROI. See the sample budget in Figure 8-1.

Often budgets need various levels of approval (authority) for signing bills and entering revenue. The authority levels should be established when the budget is developed so there are no difficulties with invoice approvals when payment is due. If you are not the signing authority for checks, who is? Also, who covers when that person is not available?

A budget must be current to be useful. Log all revenues received and expenses paid as they occur. There are two types of accounting in the budget process. They are cash accounting and accrual accounting.

Cash Accounting

Cash accounting is the logging in of revenues and expenses when they are actually received. Revenue is added to the budget when the check is received and is deposited in the account. Expenses are not deducted until an invoice is actually received and paid. This method of accounting does not take into consideration any revenues that have been provided or invoices that are expected based on contractual agreements. Therefore, cash accounting is not as good a road map as accrual accounting, but it is simpler.

Accrual Accounting

Accrual accounting takes into consideration revenues and expenses that are anticipated. They are accounted for in the month in which

Figure 8-1.   Sample budget (actual income and expense activities are not shown; these figures are hypothetical).

Line Item	Line Totals	Total Revenue	Total Expenses	Net Income
Revenues				
Registration fees				
100 ppi × $1,000	$100,000			
Sponsorship	$5,000			
Souvenir sales	$5,000			
Guest attendance				
15 ppi × $500	$7,500			
Total Revenue		$117,500		
Fixed Expenses				
Brochure design	$2,000			
Brochure printing	$10,000			
Brochure mailing	$6,000			
Speakers' fees	$10,000			
Admin. overhead	$30,000			
Space rental	$5,000			
Fees and permits	$500			
Total Fixed Expenses			$63,500	
Variable Expenses				
Breakfast				
114 ppi × $10 × 2 days	$2,280			
Lunch				
115 ppi × $15 × 2 days	$3,450			
Dinner				
114 ppi × $35 × 1 day	$3,990			
Hotel rooms				
100 rms × $100	$10,000			
Baseball caps				
115 ppi × $15	$1,725			
Program materials				
100 ppi × $50	$5,000			
Guests' scenic tour				
15 ppi × $25	$375			
Total Variable			$26,820	
Expenses		$117,500	$90,320	
NET INCOME (Return on investment)				$27,180

they are expected to be incurred. The funds for these accruals are identified so the funds are available when needed and not used elsewhere. It is similar to the way you hold funds in your personal budget to pay your rent or mortgage each month. When an accrued item is actually received, the encumbrance is removed and it becomes an actual revenue or expense.

Pace of Activity

In an effort to keep a budget out of debt (maintain a positive cash flow), it is imperative to keep a pace of activity that mirrors the pace shown in any history. For instance, if you have a four-month planning schedule for a program and the budget projects a revenue of $100,000, you should know the pace of the cash flow into the budget over that four months, based on past activity.

If previously the revenue collected was 25 percent (or $25,000) the first month, 50 percent (or $50,000) the second month, and another 25 percent (or $25,000) the third month, then your goal should be to take in 100 percent of the revenue by the third month of planning. This is important since you most likely designed the expenses to be paid out based on revenue taken in.

If revenue is behind, you would want to control costs, especially variable costs. You may choose to push more money into marketing to increase revenue from registrations. Many factors can affect your pace. It may be a holiday, a competitive industry event, or a late mailing. Whatever the cause, you need to curtail expenses so that the financial goals of the program are attained.

You should review your budget frequently throughout the program planning process. It is recommended that the budget be updated and reviewed weekly. Do not let budgets or the process intimidate you. Budgets are not fixed forever in time; they are a working tool.

Remember that a budget is just like that road map. Unless you open it and refer to it frequently throughout the journey, you really will not know where you are or where you are going.

Glossary

accrual accounting   An accounting method that treats money as income when it is earned, even though it may not actually have been received, and money to be paid out as an expense whenever bills are incurred.

administrative overhead   General overhead expenses incurred by a department but shared with administrative staff working on many different programs; calculated on an annual basis and charged back to the programs planned by the department.

budget   An estimate, often itemized, of expected income and expenses; a plan of operations based on such an estimate.

budgeting   The process of creating documents (budgets) that attempt to accurately project income and expenses for a program or series of programs.

budget revenues   Credits to a budget; cash intake.

cash accounting   An accounting method that treats money as income only when it is received, and money going out as an expense only when bills are actually paid.

fixed expenses   Program debits that will remain constant no matter how many people attend.

line items   The title of each account within a budget; usually identified by a code number.

pace of activity   Intervals at which a budget or registration is audited to see how "the numbers" are coming in compared to historical data.

return on investment (ROI)   The return the company has made, based on its investment in a program.

variable expenses   Program debits that will fluctuate based on the number of people in attendance.

zero-based budgeting   A management tactic requiring justification of all line expenditures prior to budget approval.

9

Audiovisual Materials

It has been said that with audiovisual (AV) performance, it is not noticed until there are errors. You will be expected to know what equipment you will need for your meeting, how to use the equipment to best advantage, how to assess the space available, and how to consult and confer with the audiovisual experts.

Basic Audiovisual Requirements

With technology expanding at an unprecedented rate, you need to be pragmatic. You have to know what the best technology is and who will provide it within the stated budget. Working with a reliable AV company is critical. Selection is everything! Experience counts!

The audiovisual team that gets my vote is the team that operates as a "perfect 10" every time. There is no margin for error in AV performance. Since practice makes perfect, you should choose vendors with the most experience.

Search for an AV company whose standards match yours. Know what you want and what questions to ask; keep meticulous track of recommendations and performance in order to make the best selection.

From small and medium-size vendors who own their own company (and equipment) to the large, known in-house AV companies, the success of your program depends largely on the quality of the technicians. One AV company I know has designated "A" teams and "B" teams that are sent on-site to work for clients. My concern? Only to ensure qualifying for and securing the "A" team for our jobs. Point is, here it is important to know what the criteria are for assignment of teams.

Appropriate dress of the technicians is also important. Their style of dress should match that of the audience; for example, nothing less than slacks, jacket, and tie may be required. Remember, AV personnel will be interacting with the speakers and VIPs throughout the program.

Responsibilities of the Audiovisual Company

Responsible for projection needs, an AV company arrives early the morning of the program (four to five hours prior to start time) to do the following:

- Install screen and equipment stands with pullout telescope legs.
- Place the 35mm carousel slide projector or overhead projector on one or more stands.
- Dress (with pleated skirts) the stands.
- Flip the switch to determine how high the lights should be (hopefully the room is equipped with dimmers).
- Check the ceiling for permanent spotlights in the front of the room (which create light spillover on the screen).
- Call a houseman to eliminate the spotlight (if it exists).
- Wire the room for sound (either through the house system or with a portable system).
- Wire a microphone (either handheld, on a gooseneck, or lavalier) to the lectern.
- Double-check that the projectors are in operation (either from the lectern, with control in the hands of the speaker, or by a hired technician near the projector in the rear of the room who will respond to "Next slide please!").

After a last-minute double check of the slide tray supply, the speaker-ready room, and the light and pointer on the lectern, it is show time.

While it appears that the AV company works independently, they do not. They are a member of your team. Long before setup, they must understand your needs. Then they are better able to make equipment recommendations, adjust the technology so objectives are met, and provide seamless AV for the meeting.

Here's an example. A planner placed an order for a meeting that included a screen, a pointer, a Caramate slide viewer for speakers, a 35mm projector with carousel slide tray, and a stand. However, no backup projector or additional carousel slide trays were on the list. A partnering AV company will take the initiative and suggest it might be prudent to order additional carousel slide trays and a backup projector (in case the lamp blows out). It is much quicker to replace the projector with another than to attempt to replace a hot bulb during a lecture. The company will also know when it is cost-effective to switch from monitors to a video projector. The recommendations and collaboration are invaluable to even the most seasoned planner.

New Audiovisual Technology

Computers, the Internet and intranets, audio- and videoconferencing, fiber optics, integrated services digital network (ISDN) lines, video projectors, LCD panels, and videophones are now being used. When you consider what new technologies are developed and introduced in the meeting market on an almost daily basis, the indicators point to increased reliance on the AV company. It is a good idea to periodically set aside a few hours with the AV company to review meeting needs and to ensure that programs run smoothly and cost-effectively.

Audiovisual equipment is expensive; however, it is important that your AV vendor invest in the most current equipment available. The cost of labor is a main component of AV costs and differs greatly from city to city.

New equipment, in perfect working order and supported by knowledgeable technicians who are comfortable with every aspect of the equipment, should be your standard.

Videoconferencing capabilities are no longer limited to state-of-the-art conference centers. Now available in hotels and corporations, the videoconference technology can be used in small board meetings, training sessions, and even general sessions. Videoconferencing is less expensive than satellite conferencing, and ISDN lines permit integration of computer and video. ISDN allows for faster transmission of data over telephone lines and has come down in price. ISDN-based videoconferencing is becoming available in numerous conference hotels.

Major corporate training programs embrace videoconferencing in order to train employees at multiple sites. It is also used for staff meetings or project meetings when the staff is located at multiple sites.

New products appear every day. One new product enables a desktop videoconference meeting of hundreds of participants (up to 1,000) to log on via the Internet or intranet from different sites. From the primary site, text, audio, and video can be transmitted simultaneously to all the users who are logged on.

Current information (and it changes rapidly) is reported in several of the industry publications. Contact them directly for videoconference technical information. Refer to *Corporate Meetings & Incentives* and *Medical Meetings*, published by Adams Business Media, and *Meeting News*, published by Miller Freeman. Review these and other industry publications periodically to stay on top of new developments. (See Resources at the end of the book under Meeting Publications.)

Back to Basics (Almost)

Even though there is much sophisticated equipment and new training systems and processes, the basic categories in AV remain the same: the screen/projection, the lighting, the sound, and the room setup.

Screen/Projection

Arrange the screen so that it is at an angle that makes it possible for the speaker to see the screen without turning his or her head away from the lectern microphone. The height of a room is the strong determinant of screen size. Ballroom chandeliers sometimes obstruct the projected image and have an impact on screen size and setup.

The bottom of the screen should be no less than forty-eight inches from the floor. Placing the screens on risers will add twelve to fifteen inches to the bottom height, which is preferable, especially if the room is long and narrow. When the room is long and narrow, the attendees seated in the back of the room need to look over the heads of those in front of them. Only if the screen is placed high enough (on the risers) will they have a clear field of vision.

Kinds of Projection

Front screen projection provides an excellent quality image on the screen, but the projector is generally placed on the conference room floor near the attendees. Projectors have fan units for cooling; these units are noisy. Therefore, provide enough distance between the projector and the seating area to avoid most of the noise.

Rear screen projection is set behind the screen and is not visible from the conference floor. It usually requires a space of twenty feet behind the screen. While not as clear as front screen projection, it makes a clean presentation as all equipment is out of sight. It also allows for better viewing in a room with brighter light than front screen projection.

Video monitors are selected based on the size of the monitor and the number of people in the audience. This visual enhancement is best used in a workshop or small group setting. There should be one monitor for every twenty-five to fifty people, depending upon the size of the monitor. Quality of the monitors varies tremendously. Check the quality and discuss with the vendor before ordering. When making a presentation to a large group (over 200 persons), using a video projector system with large screens is a better way to project the image.

Lighting

Most newer conference rooms are equipped with dimmers. Dimmer switches allow for more subtle adjustment of lights than the on/off switch. It is best if the dimmer control is in the same room as the meeting and easily accessible. In older hotels, where a large ballroom is divided into smaller conference rooms, the control may be in one of the other rooms.

Lights should be low enough to permit good visual definition on the screen, but not so low that attendees are unable to take notes. Remember that rear screen projection allows for more light than does front screen projection, but it uses more space. An often-forgotten light is the one on the lectern. Without it, in a darkened room, the speaker will have a difficult time reading his or her notes.

Stage lights and spotlights are generally set to highlight the speaker or panel of speakers on stage or at the lectern. The lighting should be tested and settings agreed upon prior to the meeting date, in case adjustments need to be made. While getting the right lighting can be expensive and labor-intensive (especially with more elaborate productions), it is a crucial component to the meeting's success.

Sound

Sound must be audible to all. Test the in-house system for quality and flexibility. House systems usually offer adequate sound for speeches. However, from time to time, there is a sound spillover, and you may want to address this early. Frequently the air walls (dividers), which separate one room from another in a very large ballroom, are inadequate for eliminating sound spillover. Also, check the room for dead spots (areas where the acoustics do not permit clear hearing as in other parts of the meeting room).

If you are in a room that requires the installation of a portable sound system, test the system to determine its quality. Poor sound will have a negative impact on a meeting.

Listed below are six microphone options:

Types of Microphones

1. *Lavalier microphone.* This type is hung around the neck or clipped on clothing. It permits the speaker to turn his or her head or move about if there is a long enough extension or lead.
2. *Handheld microphone.* A traditional microphone, it must be held near the mouth.
3. *Lectern microphone.* Supported and attached to the lectern via a flexible gooseneck, this type limits movement of the speaker.

4. *Table microphone.* This is used for panel discussions and/or when speakers are seated.
5. *Floor microphone.* Usually set on the floor in an aisle, this microphone is on an adjustable metal stand with a long cord, which permits the speaker to move.
6. *Roving microphone.* This is a handheld microphone, with or without an electrical cord.

Lavalier and handheld microphones can be wired or cordless. If using a cordless microphone, you should carefully test it in the specific room in which it will be used because interference is often a problem.

For beginning speakers, nervous speakers, or those simply unaware of the outcome of moving away from the microphone, it is preferable to outfit them with a lavalier or lapel microphone.

Room Setup

There is often a mix-up of the terms *podium* and *lectern*. Here is an easy way to remember which is which: The podium is what you stand on; the lectern is what you lean on.

The front of the room is where the speakers, podium, and screens are placed. A hotel ballroom may or may not be equipped with a stage. In a large room that requires a platform for a speaker or a panel of speakers, a stage or platform may be constructed. Hotels are also equipped with portable risers, ranging in height from twelve inches to three feet. The number and placement of the risers depends on the size of the room and what is to be placed on the risers. (The risers, set together, form a stage.) The arrangement to be placed on the risers (stage) may be as simple as one or two screens and a lectern for the speaker, a moderator and a panel, or any other variation of speakers and equipment.

There are several ways to arrange a room:

Basic Room Arrangements

   • *Auditorium style.* Rows of chairs facing front, with a wide center aisle. The plus is the maximum seating this style provides in a given area. The negative is that attendees do not have a place to rest materials or a table on which to take notes. (See Figures 9-1 and 9-2.)

- *Classroom style.* A room set with tables and chairs arranged either in a series of straight rows or in a chevron (**V**) shape. Classroom setup varies, based on the size of the tables. Most facilities have 6-foot or 8-foot tables; these are usually 15 inches, 18 inches, 24 inches, or 32 inches wide. This setup offers considerable flexibility to adjust the arrangement to the number of square feet in the room and the number of attendees. (See Figures 9-3 and 9-4.)

- *Crescent style.* A room set with round or oval tables. Only one side of the tables is set with chairs so all participants face the front of the room. The round tables are usually 6 feet in diameter. (See Figure 9-5.)

- *Hollow square style.* Setup of tables with no open end. Chairs are placed on the outside of the tables. The leader or group moderator sits at the table with the other conferees or attendees. (See Figure 9-6.)

- *Horseshoe or U-shape style.* Setup of tables with all connecting except one end. Chairs may be placed on the outside only or on both sides of the table. (See Figure 9-7.)

For large groups (1,000 or more), the auditorium chevron works well. In this setting, staging is necessary as it would be impossible to clearly see a speaker onstage from the rear seats. Staging should be constructed with large screens placed on either side of the stage to magnify the speaker. The screens should be angled toward the center stage for optimum viewing by the audience. (See Figure 9-8.)

Audiovisual Needs of Speakers

Your speakers may or may not be professional. To ensure the best in sound and projection, guide your speakers. Many professional speakers and trainers are comfortable with a handheld microphone. For the professional speaker, adhere completely to his or her requests for AV equipment and setup. For the nonprofessional speaker, coaching or assistance may be needed.

Provide the speakers with a speaker-ready room, which is equipped with a projector and small screen or an automatic slide viewer (fre-

(text continues on page 118)

Figure 9-1. Auditorium style (regular).

LEGEND

EP Electric pointer
REM Slide projector remote control
LAV Lavalier microphone
OH Overhead projector on cart
SLP Slide projector
PRS Projection stand

Figure 9-2. Auditorium style (chevron).

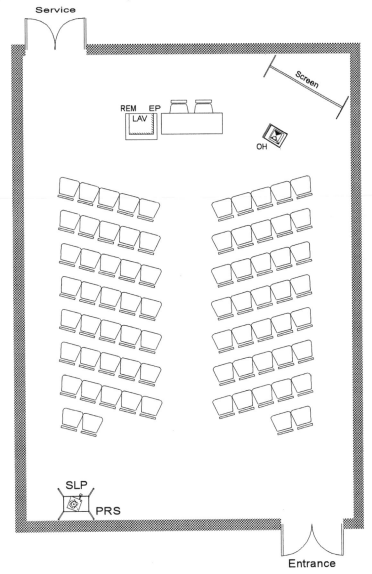

Figure 9-3. Classroom style (regular).

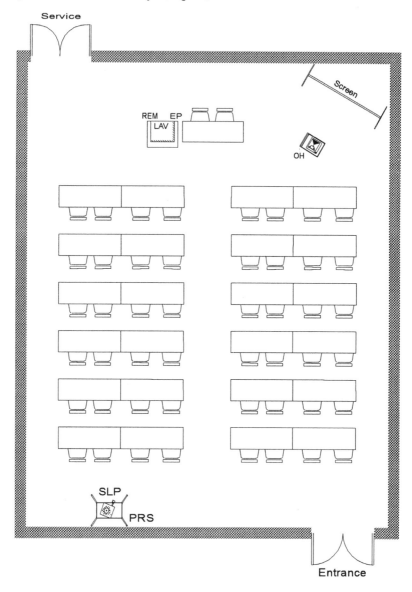

Figure 9-4. Classroom style (chevron).

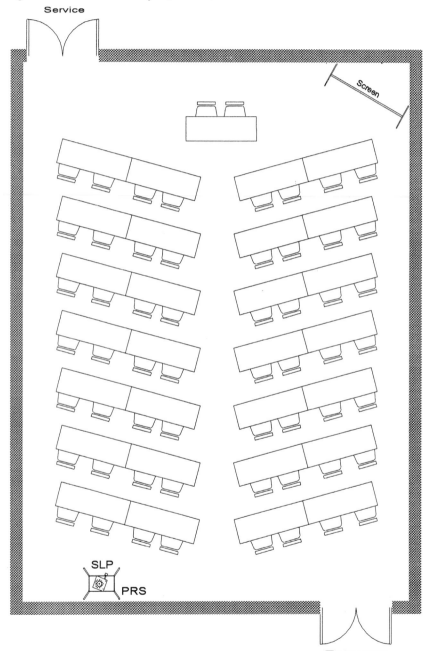

Figure 9-5. Crescent style.

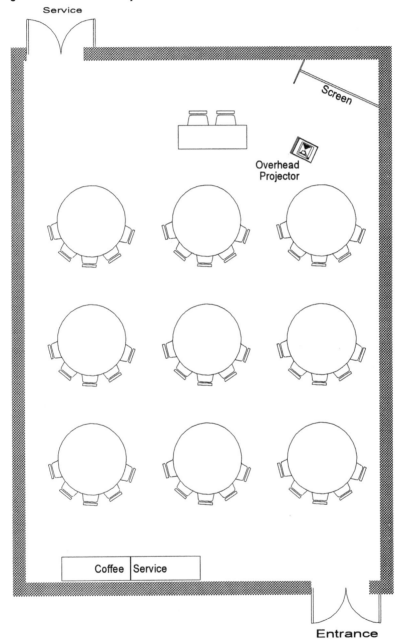

Figure 9-6.   Hollow square style.

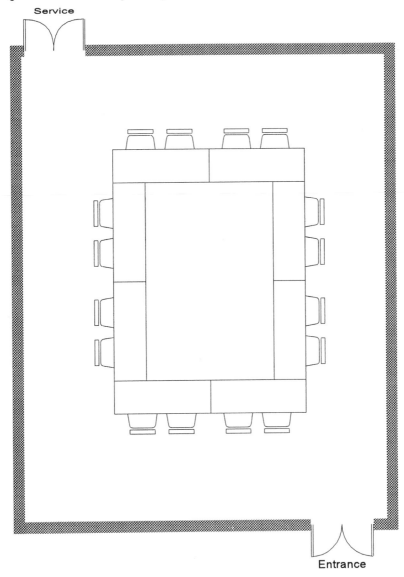

Figure 9-7. Horseshoe or U-shape style.

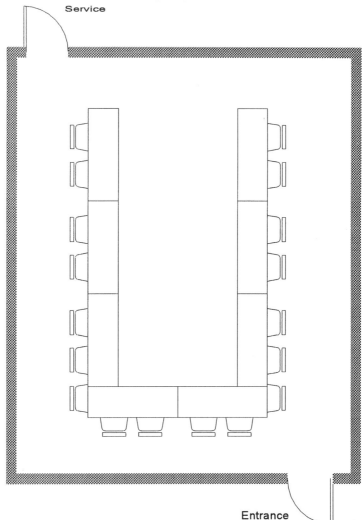

Service

Entrance

quently called a Caramate). This will permit the speaker to prepare or review his or her presentation, to check everything from content to the slides being right side up. Provide extra slide trays for the speaker. If the slides are glass-mounted, they will not fit into slide trays (carousels) that hold 140 slides because they are thicker than the cardboard-mounted slides; therefore, order slide trays that have 80 slots rather than 140, to avoid problems.

Figure 9-8. Auditorium style (chevron) for large group.

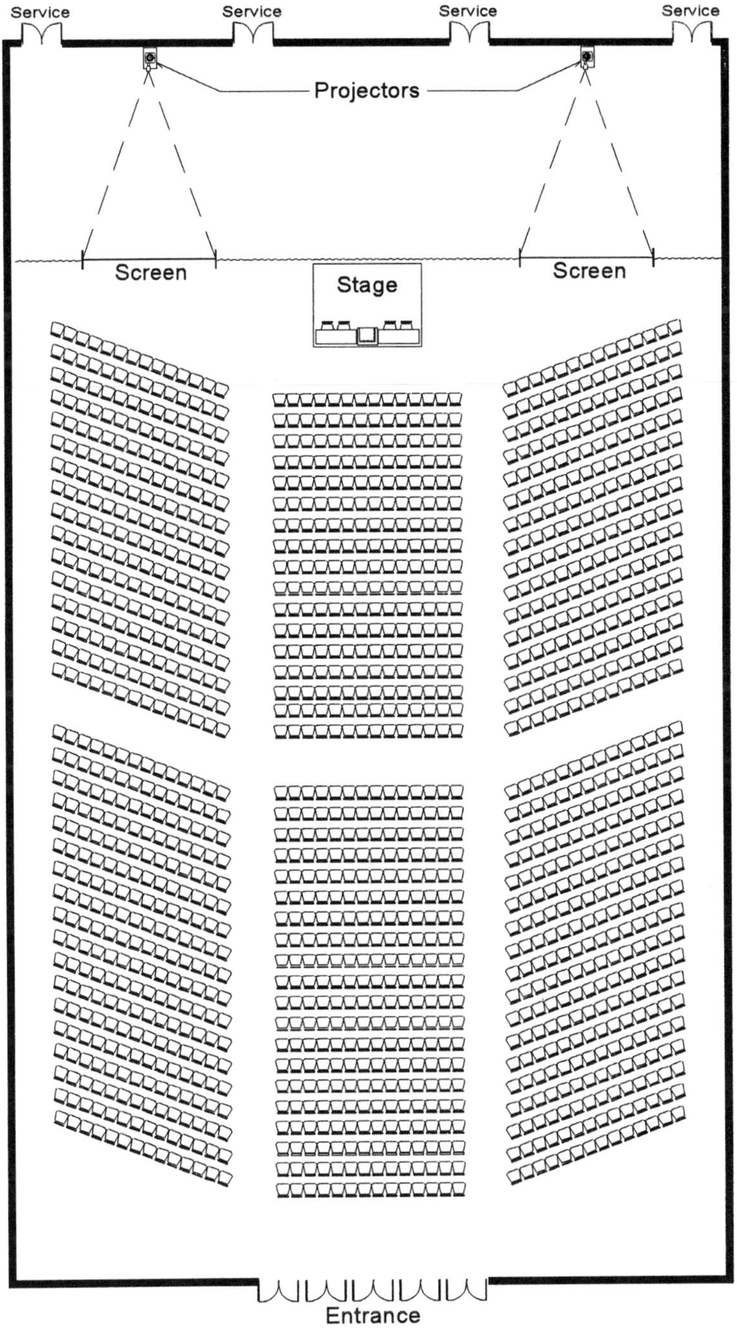

In addition to notepads and pencils, extra copies of the program, and any pertinent course information, the room should have all the necessary technical equipment as well as amenities, tables and chairs, a telephone, some bottled water, and/or coffee—in essence, it should be a mini-conference room.

It is important to note that you should contact the speaker and ask what type of presentation he or she will make. The following checklist will help you gather the information the audiovisual technicians will need to ensure speaker equipment compatibility.

Checklist—Audiovisuals
Information to Gather From Presenters
☐ Will you bring mounted slides that require a carousel tray?
☐ Will you make your slides in your own software program, such as PowerPoint?
☐ Which software program do you use for slides?
☐ Will you bring your own laptop computer, preloaded with your presentation?
☐ What type of computer will be used? (Appropriate cables must be provided.)
   ☐ PC?
   ☐ MAC?
   ☐ Sun?
☐ Will you project live video or videotapes?
☐ Will you require a flip chart?
☐ Will you require a lavalier microphone with lead?
☐ Would you prefer a wireless microphone?
☐ Will you require a technician, or will you operate your own equipment?

Items to Discuss With the Audiovisual Company
☐ Number of people in audience
☐ Size of room
☐ Meeting style (classroom, theater)

- ☐ Video monitors
- ☐ Video projector
- ☐ LCD projector requirements
- ☐ Data resolution (for viewing the program)
- ☐ The exact program
- ☐ The speakers' names and telephone numbers (to coordinate equipment needs)
- ☐ Presence of AV company technician (to assist in the slide preview in the speaker-ready room)
- ☐ A technical rehearsal (to run through all technical aspects of a show)

Glossary

audio monitor   A speaker for listening to the playback of tapes or records.

audiovisual   The equipment, materials, and teaching aids used in visual and sound presentations.

automatic advance   A feature on a slide projector that automatically inserts the next slide.

AV   Audiovisual.

carousel projector   A 35mm slide projector.

carousel tray   Holds slides for the carousel projector.

cassette   A video or audio two-reel module for recording.

cordless microphone   Microphone operating without a cord for a power source.

dimmer   A device used to control lights in a room that provides varying degrees of light.

dress   Set dressing; draperies that frame the screen or the equipment stands.

dual setup   Arrangement of duplicate setups in two different locations.

feedback   Sound from the microphone and speakers that causes a loud interference noise.

flip chart   A large pad of paper on an easel for speakers to write on.

follow spotlight   A movable spotlight.

front screen projection   Projection onto a screen by a projector in front of the screen.

gaffer's tape   Fabric tape (duct or carpet tape) used to anchor cables to the floor.

house board   Switch panel from which all electrical fixtures are operated.

integrated services digital network (ISDN) lines   Require adjustment of regular telephone lines and allow for faster transmission.

laptop computer   May be PC, MAC, or SUN; now is the most common method of conveying a presentation and may be preloaded with the presentation, ready to plug into a projector at the meeting.

lavalier microphone   A microphone that hangs on the neck or is pinned to the lapel.

lectern microphone   A microphone attached to a lectern.

liquid crystal display (LCD) projector   A technology that passes bright light through an LCD grid; LCD projectors process data presentations from a computer.

monitor   A TV set with audio and video.

overhead projector   Projects an image on-screen through a transparency.

PowerPoint   A Microsoft office software program that allows presenters to make slides in their own computer.

quad box   Four electrical outlets in one box.

rear screen projection   A projector is placed behind the screen and projects onto the screen.

roving microphone   A handheld microphone that enables audience participation as it is passed around the room.

set light   Provides light behind the speakers.

smart meeting room   Videoconferencing equipment and telephones; Internet access via ISDN lines.

spotlight   A light directed on a speaker at the lectern or on an object on the stage.

standing microphone   Microphone on a stand on the floor.

table microphone   Microphone on a stand placed on a table.

teleprompter   Device that displays the script for the speaker.

tele-suite   A suite in which virtual participants appear to one another.

transmission   Electrical or light signals sent via fiber optics, satellite, or electric wires.

VCR   Videocassette recorder.

VHS   Video home system.

videoconference   The ability to hear and see (one- or two-way) the conferees in a distant location.

video projector   Allows you to project live video or videotapes on large screens appropriate to the size of the room and the audience.

VT   Videotape.

xenon lamp   A high-intensity light source.

10

Promoting Your Meeting

Whether your meeting is a directive to employees requiring attendance at a corporate function or an invitation to engage in an optional, for-fee educational seminar or annual meeting, information about the meeting or event must be forwarded to the target audience.

You may be asked to prepare literature to secure exhibitors for a convention, entice members to a monthly meeting, encourage the sales force to embrace a series of training sessions, invite select VIPs to a fund-raising event, or announce the awards for winners of an incentive sales campaign.

The promotional piece has the power to set the tone and have an effect on participant attitudes prior to the meeting. Creating anticipation and enthusiasm for the event is a prime function of the meeting announcement and promotion materials.

The form of invitation or promotion may be hard-copy printed material, E-mail, fax, telephone (telemarketing), or Internet (via a home page), or a combination of these.

The hard-copy printed promotion may be in the form of press releases, preliminary announcements such as "Hold That Date" post-cards or interoffice memos, informal invitations, or a brochure-style format.

Whatever the meeting format, information such as the meeting date, time, and place must reach the target audience. In addition to the meeting goals and objectives, a powerful agenda along with benefits of attendance must be clearly stated.

For corporate meetings with a short lead time (i.e., meetings called within a few weeks of the meeting date), established interoffice communication systems are the best tool. The promotional materials should still, however, capture the reader's attention and solicit interest. The AIDA formula offers four basic rules for attracting attention to a promotional piece:

1. *Attention.* Use anything that will make the printed piece attract reader attention, including colorful literature, dramatic photographs, or over/undersized literature.

2. *Interest.* The reader's interest is directly linked to a need, the offer of problem solutions, or a reward for services rendered.

3. *Desire.* This is activated by the offer of benefits, the "What's in It for Me?" The more reasons the reader will benefit from attendance, the better.

4. *Action.* Clear directions to make the reader act. This may be in the form of directives such as "Hold that date!" "Call and register now!" or "Mark your calendar!"

The success of any promotional strategy depends on the following five elements: copy, lists, brochure design, package, and timing.

1. *Copy.* The copy is generally a carefully structured sales message with benefits of attendance clearly outlined. For a heading, lead with a strong meeting title. This should be the best benefit; descriptive subtitles can also be effective. Provide all pertinent meeting data, including goals and objectives, promises or guarantees, and be certain the registration form or RSVP is clearly written, easy to respond to, and that there is enough room on each form for capture of complete information for the database. Copy must always be clear, concise, and lively, with focus on the message you want delivered.

Arguments range as to whether long copy or short copy is better for promotional pieces. The current consensus is that long copy is better. Much depends, however, on whether the copy is written for a self-mailer or for a letter-style promotion piece that will be enclosed in an envelope.

The design of a self-mailer requires careful copy placement as well as attention to postal regulations. Consultation with a designer, printer, and mailer—and your postmaster—is beneficial, prior to developing the promotional piece.

2. *Lists.* You will either have in-house lists (lists provided by your corporation or association) or you will need to rent lists from an outside broker for subscription-type programs. Your in-house lists must be impeccable, with accurate names, titles, and departments. Also, it is beneficial to maintain accurate databases of E-mail addresses and fax numbers for transmittal of meeting information and updates.

If you need to rent lists, you will work with and place orders with a list broker. Because it is so critical that the lists be accurate and the target audience clearly defined, you will want to work with a reputable and highly professional list broker who can walk you through the process. A call to the Direct Marketing Association (DMA) for list broker recommendations will provide the help you need. A list broker can be of great assistance, but you will want to obtain recent references from clients. In addition, you will want to ask the DMA to forward information regarding rules and regulations for list rental. It is important that clean lists be rented; a clean list is one that is at least 95 percent accurate. This means the list receives regular maintenance, and address changes are incorporated in the databases.

3. *Brochure design.* Make the printed material look professional and important enough so that it receives the desired attention. Use color if possible as well as lots of white space. White space is what you would look at as the borders or margins, and all space surrounding copy or photographs. White space enhances your copy and makes it easy to read.

If you work with a graphics designer, be sure he or she understands your company profile. Ask to see samples of his or her work. It is also important that your/the designer's selection of paper reflects the image and culture of your company and audience. Try to avoid hidden costs for unusual designs and odd-sized paper. A large photo will increase readership. Ask yourself if the front cover or first page will get attention from your intended audience.

It is important to understand that promotional pieces and strategies follow trends. These styles and fads have a serious impact on the price of paper. Check with the printer and designer to keep current with prices of various paper stock. Unless you are using an in-house print department, you should always obtain three written bids from printers. Obtain references, check samples of their work, and verify work schedules and required lead time. Create your own file of promotional pieces, and use as a reference point for good and bad ideas.

One technique used to capture attention is the application of color. Most brochures will be produced in one or two colors, as full color (four-part color) is expensive. However, if you are announcing an incentive, you will probably have to utilize air travel and may want to contact the airline of choice or (in the case of an offshore destination) the local tourist board and ask if they can provide you with "shells."

Shells are standard brochure-sized papers ($8\frac{1}{2} \times 11$ or $8\frac{1}{2} \times 14$ or 11×17) with full-color pictures of the meeting destination. There is usually no preprinted copy on the pages. If there is copy, it should be limited to a few words regarding general destination promotion, or it may be an airline logo. The pictures are strategically and artistically placed, and the remainder of the page is available for you to use for your meeting title, agenda, goals and objectives, and registration. For limited numbers of pages—generally up to 100 pieces—there is no charge. Each tourist board will have their own rate schedule for volume orders. However, the charge is nominal when compared to contracted printing for such materials.

4. *Package.* This will include the promotional piece itself, possibly a cover letter, response mechanism such as a return card and envelope, and any other pertinent material that will be enclosed in an envelope or package. The package will include any combination of creative promotion to entice the recipient to open the package, read the material, and respond. The materials must contain a strong agenda or program with excellent speakers—and an offer with punch. Consider also, if you will, creating an open door for telephone or reminder fax follow-up to solidify attendance and acceptance of the offer.

5. *Timing.* Late promotion is one of the primary reasons for poor attendance and lack of interest. Even though a meeting may be

scheduled as a business event through a corporation, timely notification provides the participant with the opportunity to prepare. While it is not always possible to book meetings early, it is generally more expensive to book close to the program date as the promotion is then necessarily rushed. The rush element eliminates time to make cost-effective choices, and decisions are made without the opportunity to test a strategy or modify a strategic plan. Costs are higher for rush print jobs and for mailings, and the delivery options are fewer. Of course today, E-mail and broadcast fax are savers, and can be used to advantage in such situations.

If you opt for broadcast fax as the vehicle for promotion of your meeting, you should keep the message or invitation to a maximum of two sheets for transmittal. The design should be light so the transmittal moves through quickly, and costs are moderate. Fax designs with lots of dark areas transmit slowly and cost more, and gray backgrounds frequently make copy unreadable.

Optimum lead time for promotion varies with the meeting size and scope as well as the type of meeting and audience profile.

The following tips will help you with the successful development of meeting promotional materials.

Body Copy

- Never skimp or rush with copy writing.
- Clearly enumerate benefits of attendance.
- For emphasis, bullet the benefits.
- Use testimonials from prior meetings and evaluation forms.
- To gain interest, provide meeting updates and second- and third-wave promotions.
- Always write captions for photographs.
- Make the type easy to read; use no less than 9 point type.
- If you are selling, remember that the best word in copy is "free."
- Fill body copy with powerful action words.
- Keep copy simple and clear, and don't bury important information in some obscure section of the brochure.
- Finish copy with action directives such as "Call or fax your registration form" or "Complete the form and return it NOW!"
- Use testimonials. Select those that highlight benefits of attendance. Be certain to obtain permission to use the testimonial

and the name, title, and company of the testimonial giver to provide maximum credibility.
- Don't be afraid to back up your offers with a guarantee; it builds confidence.

Headlines

- Eighty percent of the overall message should be your headline.
- The headline may be short and clear, followed by a lengthier subhead.
- The headline should contain action words or problem-solve.
- Don't hesitate to use your best benefit for the headline.
- Remember that you only have seconds to capture attention with a headline.

The Registration Form

- Strive for strategic placement of the registration form.
- If possible, place it immediately below the benefits followed by an action directive.
- Lay out the form clearly with instructions to "please print."
- Provide enough line space for legible handwritten information.
- As the registration form is your data collector, design it to capture all pertinent information.

Brochure Design

- Use oversized literature to gain more attention.
- Have one important photograph on a page rather than two or three small photographs.
- Remember that press size and your finished product size will affect your overall price.
- For fund-raising, do not create literature that looks overly expensive.
- Make the brochure easy to read, easy to accept, and easy for response.
- Be sure your brochure includes goals and objectives, a promise or guarantee, benefits of attendance, the date, time, place, and tuition costs—all pertinent information.
- Use italics sparingly; it decreases reader speed.
- Keep brochures uncluttered.
- The type of paper affects the message; be certain it delivers your message.
- Create your own swipe file of good and bad promotional pieces.

Color

- Color will definitely get more attention; use it if possible.
- A two-color brochure will sell better than a one-color promotional piece.
- Color increases readability of captions.
- Color photographs increase reader interest. (Always provide captions for pictures.)
- Color headlines capture attention.
- When two colors are used, it is better to type body copy in black and accent with color to emphasize a point or more.
- When using color for headlines, the headline should be in larger and wider type to compete with the black headlines.

General Promotional Tips

- When you make promises, be sure you can deliver them.
- If a speaker is not well known, provide a comprehensive bio.
- Remember that if a photograph of a speaker will not serve as recognition, it may not have much value; copy would be better.
- Offer flexible and easy payment options.
- Track responses from the date of receipt of the first response.
- Create your budget while designing your promotion.
- Obtain a clean list guarantee from your list broker.
- Phrase cancellation clauses and penalties carefully; they may be viewed as threats.
- Consider using postcards and posters in addition to standard promotional pieces.
- Try to encourage telephone and fax registration.
- Remember that testing a new list is costly; not testing is more costly.

Checklist—Promotions

- ☐ Check with U.S. Postal Service for current mailing procedures and regulations.
- ☐ Prepare a budget for promotional materials.
- ☐ Collaborate with a professional DMA list broker.
- ☐ Review desired outcome with
  - ☐ Graphics designer
  - ☐ Printer
  - ☐ Mailer (if other than in-house)

☐ Visit
  ☐ Print shops
  ☐ Post office
  ☐ Mail houses
☐ Solicit three printing bids.
☐ Obtain paper samples.
☐ Plan a strategic approach.
☐ Review fax promotional pieces for legibility.
☐ Prepare a production sheet for timelines and deadlines.
☐ Assign proofreaders to review copy.

11

Registration and On-Site Management

Welcoming of attendees, on-site systems, staffing, on-site cash management, and good traffic flow are the ingredients for successful registration and on-site management. *Smooth, efficient, warm,* and *timely* are the operative words.

There is no second chance to make a good first impression. On-site registration is show time, and attendees, exhibitors, speakers, and sponsors who arrive for the show all have their own agenda. Each arrives with expectations; each deserves the ultimate in service.

Greeting attendees and assisting with on-site registration are important parts of the meeting's hospitality equation. The opportunity to make a positive impression begins long before the on-site registration.

From the moment meeting invitations or solicitations are sent out, invitees will have questions; they will need assistance, confirmations, instructions, guidance, and, for international programs, varying degrees of hand-holding.

The Registration Form

The simplest recommendation for development of a sufficient data collector is to look at the meeting registration form (see Figure 11-1). All information on the registration form will need to be captured in the database or registration record. If there is no registration form, consider all activities as pertinent information that may need to be submitted: the rooming list to the hotel, a list of transfers for ground

Figure 11-1.   Sample registration form.

REGISTRATION FORM

Complete and send to:
XYZ Corporation
Sales Division
1234 First Avenue
New York, NY 11111

Fee: $225.00 Corporate or Association Executive
(Registration Fee includes: course
materials, lunch & banquet)

or Fax to: 212-555-2222

My payment, in the amount of $_____, made payable to the XYZ Corporation, is enclosed for the IX Annual Conference, April 1, 2000, at the Finest Hotel, New York City, NY.

Name: _____ Title: _____
         (Please Print)

Company: _____ Street Address: _____

City: _____ State: _____ Zip: _____ Country: _____

Bus Tel: _____ Fax: _____ E-Mail: _____

Credit Card No: _____ Exp. Date: _____ Amex Visa Mastercard

Signature: _____ Date: _____

☐   I have made a reservation at the Finest Hotel
☐   I will make a reservation at the Finest Hotel
☐   I will not require a room / I have made other arrangements

transportation, a travelers' list for flight verification to the agent, or a list of tournament players for the golf pro. Whatever system is selected, it is important to adhere to the established system with one designated person responsible.

Whether your attendees were scheduled to attend (via an internal corporate mechanism) or were invited to register (via promotional materials), you will need to capture the names of each attendee. Invitations may be forwarded via direct mail, E-mail, the Internet, fax, or corporate notification within departments. The attendees' responses are important because you will need to keep track of numbers in attendance for room reservations, room seating, and food and beverage events.

Responses are most likely to be via mail, fax, or E-mail. One form for each attendee is a must; the hard-copy information received on the registration form should be captured and managed in a computer database. Software packages dedicated to registration are available; however, most computer software can be programmed to capture and manage the information presented on the registration form. This will provide you with a list of registrants (their names and titles) for printing badges and payment data.

The Processing of Registrations

Registrations should be counted, sorted, and entered into the computer on a scheduled basis. Payments, should there be any, should be noted and logged with a special notation for check, credit card, cash, or "pay later." A report of each batch of entered and processed registrations should be attached to copies of the registration forms and filed.

Whoever is designated with the responsibility of deposits will require a report, along with any checks collected for proper identification. To ensure documentation, a copy of every check (noting the payee name) should be made and attached to the report, noting the registration and payment amount. Deposit systems will vary from company to company.

Similar systems with separate records should be kept for exhibitors. The records for exhibitors will require additional fields:

- Booth assignment numbers
- Booth fees
- Number of booth (company) representatives
- Names and titles of booth representatives

After the payment is processed, the system should generate an acknowledgment or confirmation to the registrant. Absolute consistency is recommended; meticulous data input will create outstanding results while sloppy data input, inconsistent record keeping, and a case of "too many cooks" will cause problems later.

In addition to registrations for attendees, exhibitors, and speakers, there must be fields for the press, guests, sponsors, patrons, VIPs, and any participants who do not fit the general categories.

The data collected may then be sorted and used for badges, housing/ rooming lists, attendance lists, and exhibitor booth assignments. If properly set up in the beginning, any and all lists and information collected will be available in report format.

On-Site Logistics

The Registration Team

The personnel selected to perform on-site should be trained and familiar with all aspects of the logistics and registration. Each member should be provided with a scale drawing of all assigned space in the facility. Key staff should be provided with walkie-talkies for prompt communication and availability throughout the conference. Written instructions and performance expectations should be provided for everyone. Staff should be fully informed about the following:

- Schedule of events
- Times of events
- Staff assignment
- Location of vital areas (such as telephone banks, coatroom, and rest rooms)

When assembling your on-site team, some of whom may be volunteers, it will help to use the following thirteen-item checklist:

1. Assign an adequate number of registrars, with backup if needed.
2. Select the right personality for greeters/registrars. An outgoing, sunny personality with a desire to help people is a must.
3. Assign registrars who can and will smile under almost any circumstance, believe the customer is always right, and enjoy the roll to the fullest.
4. Train the on-site registration staff; training and teamwork begin in the office.
5. Be certain to assign one person as the troubleshooter. A diplomatic decision maker will best be able to calm and satisfy an angry participant.

6. Advise all on-site staff as to the dress code. Choose business attire (conservative suit, blazer) for a formal setting; if the conference is in a resort, smart or business casual may be more appropriate. Be specific so there can be no misunderstanding. Attendees, exhibitors, and speakers will all respond better to staff with professional demeanors and dress.

7. Advise all staff to wear comfortable business shoes (gum soles or cork soles are most comfortable) as their well-being is important to the function. Everyone should leave a change of shoes in the staff room for additional comfort.

8. For large conferences with a large staff, provide a special staff room. For smaller meetings, the show office may be used for the staff breaks as well.

9. If volunteers are brought on as ad hoc staff, require them to find a replacement in the event of an emergency that would preclude their attendance.

10. Stock the registration area with an ample supply of meeting programs, maps, and pertinent material available for distribution.

11. Establish boundaries and areas of responsibility. This is not meant to discourage staff support, but to eliminate confusion during busy registration periods. When the need arises, staff should cover for one another.

12. Provide every staff member with an Emergency Life Line Sheet. This sheet will contain the toll-free telephone numbers of all major airlines, taxis, and related contacts for the meeting.

13. Keep a dispatcher in the office.

Here is a sample scenario. A speaker arrives at the airport, and the scheduled car is not there. The speaker can't reach anyone in the hotel. The speaker calls the conference office only to hear a voice message that tells him or her, "Everyone is at a conference." Now consider an alternative scenario. He or she calls the office; one staff member, left behind in the capacity of dispatcher, receives the call and saves the day.

Signage

Nothing will frustrate and annoy an attendee as much as being lost (except maybe being lost and late). Somehow, the two seem to go hand in hand. Without adequate signs throughout the facility, attendees will surely lose their way. Some hotels are signage nightmares:

They are filled with corridors that twist and turn; some hallways seem to go nowhere; there is an old tower, a new tower, and lots of dead-end traps. Prepare enough signs (with arrows) and place them where needed to ensure that attendees find the conference registration area without difficulty. Directions can't be overstated; attendees will appreciate the consideration. When a hotel won't permit you to use its signs, ask them to prepare the signs in accordance with its policy, and indicate where you want them placed.

The Registration Area

The registration area must be clearly marked so that, upon arrival, the attendee knows which desk to approach. Signage in the registration area should be placed at least eight feet off the ground to make it visible above the heads of people in the area. Additional signs on easels, with directional red arrows, are also a welcome assist.

For large conferences, one or two staffers (greeters) should be at the entrance. After a brief question, they would direct the participant to the correct area. Send arriving exhibitors and speakers to different areas (space permitting), and provide them with special assistance geared to their needs.

Staffing for the Registration Area

Traffic flow must be considered. Ask the following questions:

- When will it peak?
- How many staff members will be required to handle the registration traffic prior to peak, during peak hours, and after peak hours?
- Will the participants arrive in groups by bus?
- Will they arrive two by two?
- Will they cluster at a certain hour?

At peak hours, plan for a ratio of 1 staff for every 75 to 100 attendees.

If the meeting has a history, it is best to draw on experiences and information gathered from prior meetings. If the meeting is a first-time-out program and the number of staff is an issue, it would be prudent to overstaff, even if only during peak hours.

The preconference meeting (pre-con), generally held the day or evening before the main event, will introduce and coordinate your staff with the facility staff. A good pre-con meeting will outline the responsibilities of all hotel staff who have been assigned to work your meeting, along with their regular and emergency telephone numbers. All issues should be discussed at this meeting. The convention services manager, with whom you have been working during the weeks before the conference, will be on-site and available to troubleshoot at all times during your meeting.

On-Site Registration Etiquette

The following two lists are guidelines for registration staff:

Do

- Wear an attitude that indicates you are the best person to approach for a question.
- Be prepared to solve problems. If there is confusion or a problem at the registration desk, do not detain the attendee. Indicate that you are certain you can work it out, and urge him or her to join the meeting.
- For fee-related issues (such as "The check is in the mail!"), take proper documentation (a business card, along with a credit card) and urge the attendee to participate in the meeting.
- Call your designated troubleshooter for assistance when the issues appear to be unsolvable. Do not shout for the troubleshooter; either make eye contact or bring the attendee to that person for resolution. Say, "Let me introduce you to. . . ! She/ he can help you."
- Adhere to the established dress code. Attendees, exhibitors, and speakers will all respond better if you look professional.
- Wear comfortable business shoes (gum soles or cork soles are most comfortable).
- Carry few personal items and leave those you do bring with you in the show or staff office.
- Maintain the preassigned staffing schedule, but call for backup when needed.
- Be willing to provide a substitute or replacement in the event of an emergency that would preclude your keeping the commitment.

- Memorize all the information provided in the Emergency Life Line Sheet so you can assist those who approach you.
- Be prepared to become a human arrow as you appropriately direct attendees to telephone banks, coatrooms, meeting rooms, and rest rooms.
- Smile at all times.
- Enjoy the assignment.

Do Not

- Do not engage in personal conversation while at the registration desk. One never knows who may hear the conversation.
- Never make negative comments about registrants, the program, the exhibitors, or the facility. If you can't say something nice. . . .
- Do not place food or drink on the registration desk.
- Avoid chewing gum, using slang, or making jokes. Innocent comments and laughter may be misinterpreted by those whose first language is other than English.
- Do not indulge in negative responses to a registrant, exhibitor, or speaker (even if they appear warranted).
- Do not sit while speaking to attendees; stand and greet them with a smile and a positive attitude.

On-Site Tipping

The on-site staff is the front line of defense. Working with the facility representatives and staff, the vendors (outside AV company, florist, musicians, guest speaker), and all the on-site partners is a formidable task. In addition, there is one more, and though it may seem easy, it causes much concern to the planner: the responsibility of payment through tips. Reward and recognition through tips is a large variable. Tipping can be tricky because there are no standards. Surveys (there have been many) show that there are planners who never tip, those who tip moderately, and those who tip a great deal. How one tips is another question. Does one tip along the way? Or is it appropriate to tip at the conclusion of the program? The rule is . . . there is no rule!

How Much Should You Tip?

The main tipping questions are (1) How much? and (2) When is a tip a bribe? In the United States, a tip is expected; it is not considered a bribe. A generous tip is an indication of a job well performed, with timely extra service provided. The meeting industry is a service-related industry, and tipping is an important part of the service compensation picture.

In hotels, we know we are expected to tip bellmen, package room personnel, housemen, bell captains, room service, housekeepers, concierge, front desk managers, sales directors, and convention services managers.

Tips may be cash tips, payouts (tips arranged for through the master account), or gifts. An additional tip may be the letter of commendation, which is not in lieu of the cash tip or gift but which is an appreciated additional tip. This would generally be for the convention services manager, his or her staff (if there are any), and the sales office that helped you get started. A letter of appreciation and commendation to the immediate supervisor or employer of the convention services manager or the sales director (with a cc on the letter to the employee) is not just a letter of thanks, but it carries weight for promotions and salary increases; it is, in effect, a tip.

Who Should Be Tipped?

The bellmen, bell captain, and package room personnel deserve a tip, based on their performance. Also tip the doorman (when he hails a cab), the chambermaid (daily as shifts change), and room service personnel. On average, $1 to $2 per item, per incident, with $2 per night for the chambermaid, are current, loose guidelines.

Remember food and beverage prices come with a plus-plus charge. This is the charge for gratuity and tax and varies considerably from location to location. We assume that the waiter/waitress staff receive the gratuity. However, in many instances, they receive only a percentage of a charged gratuity. Some facilities distribute a portion of the gratuity to supervisory personnel; management may even receive the balance. This is sometimes outlined on the reverse side of printed food and beverage menu listings.

In addition to the required gratuity (which varies from state to state), most of us feel it beneficial to tip the captain/headwaiter and, of course, any support staff who have provided service during the program, such as housemen, bartenders, and AV staff. How much to tip is the question. Some prefer to tip a flat fee for service rendered; others prefer a percentage of the bill, which will be divided into increments and distributed according to rank and service provided.

Checklist—Registration

☐ Develop registration system or select suitable registration software.

☐ Enter data: Conference name, dates, location, tracks, social events, exhibitors, speakers.

☐ Enter registrants: Name, company, address, telephone, fax, E-mail, fee, payment method.

☐ Process for payment: Reports, deposit slips, credit cards.

☐ Forward confirmations, acknowledgments, and/or appropriate communications regarding receipt of registration.

☐ For those who owe money, prepare special correspondence on a regular basis until paid or in accordance with the stated agreement.

☐ For cancellations, refunds, and other customer services, retrieve records, enter requested charges, acknowledge, and process refund if required.

☐ Print badges.

☐ Prepare on-site registration lists.

☐ Prepare and/or include in on-site packages the certificates of attendance.

☐ Prepare/train on-site registration volunteer staff, adhering to policies.

☐ Review on-site logistics, signage, and traffic flow.

☐ Prepare supply of registration forms for on-site completion by walk-in attendees (those not previously registered).

☐ Process on-site registrations.

☐ Process all monies collected on-site.

☐ Check collections and do cleanup: Letters to no-shows and to those who still owe money (requesting payment).

☐ Do the final accounting, reconciliation, and reports.

12

International Meetings

International meeting responsibilities range from site selection to "making it happen." When asked to select a site via fax and/or E-mail, without benefit of a site visit, partnerships become invaluable.

International partnerships may be with national tourist offices, Convention and Visitors' Bureaus, hotel and facility representatives, airlines, destination management companies, tour operators, professional congress organizers, or suppliers in the business of marketing their country and services to the meeting industry.

Partnerships provide an inexhaustible source of information. As incoming meetings are important business for many countries, the destination representatives (airlines, government-supported tourist boards, hotels) are extremely supportive and will work diligently to assist with booking your group. However, no commitments should be made until after the final determination that a country and venue will accomplish the established goals and objectives of the meeting.

What you will be most concerned with are the differences in operation in other countries. At a recent conference, a European hotel representative observed that Americans believe there are two countries in this world: the United States and International.

When creating your checklists for international meetings, you must address the differences in each country and make adjustments. Note and compare what and how we do it here versus what we must do there in order to provide a successful international program.

Rationale

Will the meeting be a corporate incentive? Product launch? Meeting to provide interaction with corporate members from overseas? Educational meeting? Or an annual association meeting? Considerations include budget, planning timetable, program design, ease and safety of transportation, and risk management.

Is it a popular destination? Is the travel time reasonable (for this meeting)? Will it be possible to work in that specific environment? It's interesting to note that exotic destinations are attractive to the potential attendees; these are also the destinations that are more difficult to navigate for that very same reason. For example, is the food so exotic that menu preparation becomes a problem for a substantial number of participants?

Are language and customs issues surmountable? How will this destination impact on the budget? Can a suitable contract be negotiated? How will issues of currency, protocol, and safety and security be handled? In many countries, the travel, tourism, and hospitality industry is big business. For example, in Switzerland, tourism is one of the three major revenue sources, and each major area (canton) competes for business. This is much the same as in the United States where cities, such as New York, Washington, D.C., and Boston, compete for business.

Incentives and group travel, meetings, conferences, and trade shows are substantial revenue streams. The national tourist offices (NTOs) are always searching for decision-making planners or planners who make site recommendations. They will greatly assist those who have the potential to bring group business to their country.

Information Gathering

Information (for your fact sheet) about offshore destinations may be obtained from the International Association of Convention and Visitors' Bureaus, or you may call the Department of Commerce (DOC) in Washington, D.C. Identify the country in question; ask for the desk officer of that country. The desk officer will provide a comprehensive report and/or fact sheets about the following:

- Social customs for doing business
- Business matters (workweek, calendar, language)
- Health
- Religion
- National information (population and size)
- Government (the legal system)
- The economy (current exchange rate and the import/export situation)
- Social information (such as forms of greeting, nonverbal communication, manners, dining customs, conversation styles)
- Travel information

Sound basic? Just good old common sense? You are right! However, it's the little things that trip us up. My first week-long meeting in Spain was for Pediatricians from the U.S.A. We were in an outstanding four-star hotel on the beautiful Costa Del Sol. Food was excellent, service was impeccable, and I was Public Enemy Number One.

Why? I had not gathered complete information about the destination. Physician groups traditionally begin their day early. This program seemed no different. I began the program at 7:45 A.M. and concluded the day's session at 1:00 P.M. (preparing for a close that would allow time for touring and shopping each day). Two glaring errors haunted me all week. The first was that the attendees were released from the educational sessions and given an opportunity to go shopping just when the stores closed for the afternoon. The second error was that abominable start time. In Spain, it is not unusual to dine at 10:00 P.M. Well, if you begin dining at 10:00 P.M., you finish close to midnight. If you go to bed immediately (and most wanted to have some leisurely conversation after dinner) and must rise for a 7:45 A.M. start. . . ! Need I say more. A quick call to the Department of Commerce and a check on local customs would have saved me from these errors.

EventPlanner is an additional information source, which can be found on the Internet: http://www.eventplanner.com/cities/europe/

uk.htm. As with the DOC, it will provide country and city profiles of numerous locations; however, it does not yet have as complete a listing as the Department of Commerce.

The U.S. State Department Web site provides travelers with the latest global news, current tips, and travel warnings. (See the Resources at the end of this book under International Meetings.)

Incentive meetings have selected international locales as the optimum reward for attendees for many years. Today, American corporations and associations are taking meetings offshore in greater numbers than ever before, and the trend is expected to continue. However, the design of the incentive meeting, in many instances, has changed. Small incentive groups (with spouses) are now combined with training events, and when the sponsoring corporation is a multinational corporation, it may offer an opportunity to interact with and build better business relationships abroad.

Budgeting
Travel Expenditures

Travel expenditures can increase significantly for international meetings. Corporate guidelines may provide for travel upgrades to business or first class, if the flight is longer than six hours, for speakers, VIPs, and/or staff. Though the picture varies from time to time, airlines currently offer small discounts for incentives and group travel, and they require a deposit when the contract is signed.

Air Expenses for Inter-European Travel

Because the point-to-point distance from one country to another in Europe is so insignificant compared with distances in the United States, it is easy to think airfares will be less expensive. This is not always true. Actually, the cost of inter-European travel may be more expensive than a flight from New York, Boston, Washington, D.C., or even from San Francisco. However, since the deregulation of 1997/1998, there are new low-cost carriers, lower fares, and more service to secondary cities. A good alternative to air travel are the high-speed train services, which are reliable and popular in many countries. Calculate the time factor; then take a look at schedules to assess this possibility.

Additional Nights

Jet lag is a reality. Additional nights may be required to allow VIPs, speakers, and participants to recoup before the meeting starts. Time should be slotted for locale orientation; don't underestimate the need for familiarization with new counterparts (those with whom you will do business).

Postal Costs

E-mail and fax have done more to control this line item in the budget than any other single factor. However, shipping costs always seem to exceed the budget; this is driven by materials that are too voluminous to be faxed and must be sent overnight. Privatized services are available in most areas. Check their individual services to obtain one that suits your needs in your specific destination.

Translation Expenses

Simultaneous translation or simultaneous interpretation (SI) may be required. It is expensive but necessary for meetings where the delegates are unable to communicate in one language. Some meetings will state that the meeting will be conducted in one language. However, it is not logical to expect international participation and not provide delegates with the opportunity to hear scientific or professional information comfortably in their own language. Attendees are your guests; although it is expensive, it is basic courtesy to provide SI.

Simultaneous Interpretation

Simultaneous interpretation is the same system as that used by the United Nations. The speaker's remarks are translated into any number of languages and broadcast to the listeners on their own selected channel in their designated language. For example, channel 3 might be in English; if attendees wanted to hear the English translation, they would flip their individual control to that channel (no. 3) and hear English on their individual headsets.

There are a few important requirements for the setup of the SI system. Additional rental time of the facility is needed as it takes a day to set up this portable system. Simultaneous interpreters companies are heavily booked; it is imperative to reserve their services as early as possible, no less than a year out. The SI company of choice will advise regarding the setup. To be very prudent, avoid booking your space until after you have consulted with the SI company with regard to space requirements. They will set soundproof booths in the meeting room and create the proper environment for your meeting.

SI is more readily available as a number of newer convention and conference centers have built-in SI systems, including soundproof booths. Check this variable as a plus when booking a facility.

For best results, do not hire translators from government organizations, universities and research groups, or large translation agencies. The best translators are copywriters at professional advertising agencies and people in your specific industry.

Even with professional translation, some words and phrases do not translate well into other languages. In the September 1997 issue of *Successful Meetings* (column by Greater Cincinnati Convention and Visitors' Bureau), it was noted that attendees from Japan were confused when the famous line "Show me the money" was translated into Japanese. The translation they heard directed them to "Display now your currency!"

However, in a *DM News International* (February 17, 1997) column by Simon Anholt, he noted that in a certain African language, the equivalent of the English expression "the tip of the iceberg" is "the ear of the hippopotamus."

While there will always be some translation errors due to language differences and idiomatic expressions, problems may be kept to a minimum by providing simultaneous interpretation. Also, when interacting with international groups, speak perfect textbook English; avoid jokes, slang expressions, and colloquialisms.

Speaker Translation Assistance

If speakers are presenting in English but have substantial accents and are generally difficult to understand, it is very helpful to the listening audience to see slides or overheads that have the basic talk printed in English. This is one of those times when we suggest that a set rule (discouraging speakers from printing their talk on the slides) be broken. The audience can easily read what is on the screen, and it eases the listening-difficulty score substantially.

Insurance (Safety and Security)

Safety and security, along with an on-site medical crisis plan, are top meeting priorities for international programs. The United States has been more secure than many other countries; until recently, we had no real history of daily terrorism. Americans have also come to take for granted sanitation and availability of instant, on-demand medical service. This is not available to the same degree in many other countries. To protect the participants and the organizers, solid risk management demands preparation from the meeting organizers. It appears that the number of international meetings will rise despite some blips due to terrorism. These acts of terrorism can happen anywhere; for the offshore meeting, it is wise to double efforts and attempt to provide a fail-safe contingency plan that identifies all risks and makes preparation to diffuse the risks. Just as the issue of liability requires the determination whether to hire counsel or not, so should a planner of an international meeting consider either consultation with or the hiring of a security specialist.

A plan for emergencies needs to be in place. Check your corporate policy, and work with the internal security department if there is one. If there is no dedicated security office, seriously consider getting help; seek the services of a security consultant.

Corporations usually have a policy for handling death, emergencies, and security issues. Your corporate policy should be reviewed prior to the event in order to plan effectively for an emergency. Who to contact if and when there is an offshore emergency and preparedness for such an event will ensure the resolution of issues in accordance with policy and, hopefully, will avoid embarrassment and legal actions.

Most airlines will provide bereavement fares at reasonable rates if an attendee has to rush home due to a death in the family. A comprehensive list of airlines and their policies is of great help in an emergency. Survey the major airlines and your group carrier for policy and procedures regarding such fares.

Currency Exchange Rates

When negotiating contracts and costing tours for a meeting planned several months out or a year out, it is unlikely that the current exchange rate will be in effect at the time of the meeting. Fluctuations in currency exchange rates are the norm. Currency moves on current events and changes daily. The challenge is how to offset any losses that may occur because of an unfavorable swing in the exchange rate.

The safest path is the most costly; however, that does not mean it is to be avoided. On the contrary, it may be a good selection. When you negotiate with a hotel and facility in American dollars, they must eventually convert the dollars to their own currency; this will cost them fees. If you do contract in U.S. dollars, be certain the exchange rate is fixed with a contract. Many hotels will negotiate in U.S. dollars; some will not. While the hotel may be willing to negotiate in dollars, there are vendors that will not. Ground operators usually will not price in U.S. dollars.

If you collect fees from your delegates (either before the program or on-site), you can deal in local currency and make exchanges with the hotel or your tour operator. If collecting checks from foreign countries, ask that they be drawn on an international bank and be in U.S. dollars. Multinational companies will have their own internal system, and this operation will be handled according to their policy.

When there is no multinational company to assist, you may opt to seek the services of one of several known international currency handlers.

In the absence of a currency supplier, use the following guidelines:

- Try to select a location with free-traded currency.
- Use your hotel facility as your bank and arrange to pay the expenses with monies collected on-site.

- Consider purchase of forward contracts.
- Decide whether to charge (when appropriate) in local currency or in U.S. dollars.

Forward contracts mean that you can lock in a current (today's) exchange rate and it remains your rate until funds are actually purchased at a later date. As a hedge, you can purchase forwards for a portion of the funds you will need for your program. There is a minimum, however; currently, it is $10,000 worth of the foreign currency.

Value-Added Tax

In most European countries and Canada, the value-added tax (VAT) is imposed on general consumer expenditures and business transactions, such as hotel rooms, food and beverage, conference or trade show fees, training courses, professional fees, and car rentals. With the exception of food and beverage, most of the imposed VAT is recoverable. Currency traders and VAT reclaim specialists (listed in the Resources at the end of this book) will provide you with forms and, for a nominal fee, will assist with the reclaim. It is unfortunate that many U.S. corporations neglect to claim VAT refunds—a costly oversight. Since the VAT can amount to 19 percent, or in Ireland 25 percent, the reclaim average of 17 percent can make a significant impact on the budget.

Individuals may also avoid paying the VAT on significant purchases such as jewelry. Store merchants will provide individuals with a form to be completed and instruct the buyer to deposit the completed form in the airport mailbox upon departure. The amounts of tax vary from country to country, just as our tax rates vary from state to state.

Note: For a valid VAT reclaim with a facility, the applicant must be the same as the signer of the contract.

Preparation of Participants

Preparing the international meeting participant is as important as the checklist we create for ourselves. It's interesting to note that while we prepare ourselves for an international meeting and develop excellent guidelines, we sometimes forget to share them with the participants.

In my experience, I find the more informed my participants are, the more forgiving and understanding they are when a glitch occurs. They like to be prepared for the climate, the dress code, special events that may require additional costumes, and variations of the climate if tours to other areas are part of the program.

What and How to Pack

Advise travelers of any baggage weight-limitation regulations; have them plan to take only one carry-on bag. Instruct them to do the following:

- Pack important medications in the carry-on bag.
- Keep medications in their original prescription bottle; under no circumstances empty several medications into one unidentified bottle or pillbox.
- Keep a copy of the prescription in either a wallet or a purse (in case of loss, illness requiring a refill, and/or the need to identify the medication).
- Be sure to pack toiletries, overnight necessities, and at least one change of clothes in the carry-on in case the checked-in luggage is delayed or lost.
- Limit the number of valuables to what you are wearing.
- Keep passport and money securely with you.

Visa, passport, and financial information rank high on the most frequently asked questions list by international meeting participants. Three copies of the passport (with a visible, light, identifiable picture of the passport holder) should be made: One should be left home (with a secretary or accessible family member); one should be packed in the carry-on or some place other than where the original is housed; and one should be given to the group leader.

Travel Information Packets

Local Information and Maps

Provide everyone with information about local customs, facility telephone use, and local and public transportation availability (for those who will go off on their own). Advise those participants who may rent cars concerning law enforcement regulations. Supply them with maps that indicate the location of the airport, the hotel, and other familiar landmarks.

Taxes

Just as the group contract is subject to the value-added tax, so are purchases made by the participants. Advise them on how they may recover the tax prior to departure; whenever possible, provide VAT reimbursement forms.

Credit Cards

It is helpful to carry an alternate to Amex, such as Diners Card, MasterCard, or Visa. Amex is unpopular in Europe, due to high service charges. While Amex may be unpopular in Europe, its Global Assist for cardholders is a service benefit. (See Resources at the end of this book.)

ATM Cards

ATM users abroad have encountered problems because the card and system are not always compatible. It is wise to have a backup resource for obtaining cash.

Hospitality Desk

The hospitality desk should be located in an accessible area of the facility: in the lobby, in a separate room just off the lobby, or in the meeting area. Wherever its location, it should be clearly marked, friendly, accessible, open for business during convenient hours (for the meeting participants and their families), and fully staffed with meeting personnel, destination management staff, and tour guides who are multilingual.

The conference organizers may staff the hospitality desk, with assistance from the national tourist office, the Convention and Visitors' Bureau, or the professional congress organizer. Use the following guidelines:

- The on-site staff should be bilingual, if not multilingual, depending on the needs of your guests.
- There should be coordination with the on-site staff and the meet/greet team at the airport.
- Reception and registration into the facility should be arranged for prior to the attendees' arrival at the hospitality desk. A welcome drink is comforting as they pick up their key.
- This preregistration provides for immediate check-in—no waiting for tired travelers; however, some facilities will not permit preregistration.
- Assistance should be provided for tours, shopping, maps, transportation, currency exchange, restaurant recommendations, VAT reclaim, and (toward the end of the conference) reconfirmation of tickets.
- Information and dining recommendations are very important to international travelers. Provide lists of restaurants, outlining their specialties and noting their price range. For example, there should be a list of reasonable, moderate, and expensive restaurants. Also be prepared to make reservations for the attendees and to assist with transportation information and taxi service.
- Some international meeting attendees bring spouses while others do not. Do remember to take care of the single traveler. Include the single traveler in nonformal dinner arrangements.

A properly staffed and stocked hospitality desk will become a home-like lounge, a haven for help and friendly support. It is a critical component of the international meeting. Studies and surveys indicate that while some of your group may be seasoned travelers who like to venture off on their own when there is time, most people attending meetings in a country other than their own prefer organized events and much guidance.

Contracts, Customs, and Protocols

Putting these together is no mistake! When attempting to employ some negotiation tactics in another country, it is imperative that the customs and protocols of the country in which business will be conducted are understood and adhered to. We Americans have a tendency to move quickly; a semi-accepted motto is: Business first, play later. However, in other countries, what appears to be play first is a device to get to know and assess you and your business. Nothing wrong with that—it makes for fewer errors.

The travel section of most bookstores will offer a variety of publications that will prepare the uninitiated traveler. Also check the Adams Business Media book mart and the book store of Meeting Professionals International for additional material. See Resources under Meeting Publications and International Meetings at the end of this book.

Checklist—Considerations for International Meeting Site

☐ Study the world globe.

☐ Call resources for information

    ☐ Department of Commerce (desk officer in specific country).

    ☐ Department of Transportation.

    ☐ National tourist office (NTO).

    ☐ Flag carriers.

    ☐ Reputable travel agents.

    ☐ Destination management companies.

☐ Purchase books on protocol in specific destinations.

☐ Check visa requirements.

☐ Review hotel options.

☐ Assess ease/difficulty of travel.

☐ Verify cost of travel.

☐ Check safety issues.

☐ Determine political and economic stability.

☐ Check general opinion of the destination.

☐ Is it English-speaking?

☐ Will it accomplish stated goals/objectives?

☐ Budget preparation.

- ☐ Additional costs for
  - ☐ Meeting room rental.
  - ☐ Printed materials.
  - ☐ Marketing/promotion.
  - ☐ Postal costs.
  - ☐ Upgraded airfares.
  - ☐ Additional room nights to overcome jet lag.
  - ☐ Translation.
  - ☐ Insurance.
  - ☐ Currency exchange.
- ☐ Destination criteria.
- ☐ Adequate air lift.
- ☐ Political climate.
- ☐ Economic climate.
- ☐ Right-to-work permit requirement.
- ☐ Weather.
- ☐ Shopping.
- ☐ Security/safety/medical assistance.
- ☐ Tourist board support.
- ☐ Tax laws.
- ☐ Banking.
- ☐ Orientation for attendees
  - ☐ Note currency fluctuations.
  - ☐ Advise VAT refund information.
  - ☐ Advise issues concerning ATM users.
  - ☐ Advise credit card preferences abroad.
- ☐ Attendee provisions
  - ☐ Passport and visa information.
  - ☐ Maps.
  - ☐ Local customs information.
  - ☐ Dress codes.
  - ☐ Small local dictionaries.
  - ☐ Taxi rates.
  - ☐ Tipping customs.

- ☐ Dining and shopping information.
- ☐ Museum passes or guides.
- ☐ Well-staffed hospitality desk.
- ☐ Multilingual staff.
- ☐ Tour guides.
- ☐ Baggage weight limitations.
- ☐ Information on how to pack for travel.
- ☐ Medical guides.
- ☐ Host committee to assist with protocols.
- ☐ Cultural differences to brief staff about.
- ☐ Business cards in two languages.
- ☐ AV in hotel outside company.
- ☐ Use of flags.
- ☐ Gift purchasing.
- ☐ Destination management company for transport and tours.
- ☐ Contract payment requirements review.
- ☐ VAT refund application.
- ☐ Embassy contact.
- ☐ Department of State contact.
- ☐ Web sites information
  - ☐ Profile of destination country.
  - ☐ Travel warnings for travelers.
  - ☐ Weather.
  - ☐ Enforcement activities.
  - ☐ Current currency rates.
  - ☐ Economics.
  - ☐ Demographics.

Checklist—Meetings at a Specific International Destination

- ☐ Consider services of airlines and/or reputable travel agents.
- ☐ Obtain assistance/information from tourist board.
- ☐ Obtain assistance/information from local destination management company.

- ☐ Request information from embassy.
- ☐ Contact hotel(s).
- ☐ Review local customs/habits.
- ☐ Identify local holidays.
- ☐ Check hours for banking, dining, shopping.
- ☐ Review local currency issues.
- ☐ Review food and beverage for restrictions.
- ☐ Research
    - ☐ Local attractions.
    - ☐ Museums.
    - ☐ Historic sites.
- ☐ Check driving rules/regulations.
- ☐ Determine if it is feasible to rent cars.
- ☐ Verify time from airport to hotel.
- ☐ Check weather conditions (time of year).
- ☐ Check VAT and departure tax.

Glossary

ASTA   American Society of Travel Agents.

back to back   Meetings scheduled so that one group departs, another arrives in that destination.

bereavement fares   Fares for immediate family members of newly deceased.

boarding pass   A part of your ticket with your seat assignment and which permits you to board an aircraft.

bulkhead   The dividing section of a cabin. The seats facing that section are bulkhead seats.

business class   The class of seating between first class and coach.

carnet   An official document permitting materials to be shipped into another country and also to be returned to the United States—a right of passage for goods for which you must make application.

charter flight   An aircraft that has been chartered for the exclusive use of one group.

coach   Seating in majority of an aircraft. Also called "economy."

concierge   Special designated staff in a facility. They provide special services to guests.

Convention and Visitors' Bureau (CVB) Provides services for the meetings and conventions industry and promotes their specific destination.

delegates The international term for attendees or meeting participants.

Department of Commerce (DOC) A country-by-country resource for demographic information.

Department of Transportation A resource for public transportation information such as "fly rights" for passengers engaging in travel.

departure tax A tax imposed on travelers departing from a country.

destination management company (DMC) A local on-site management company.

duties Tax imposed on goods shipped from one country to another.

exchange rate The variance in currency from one country to another.

familiarization trip (Fam trip) A familiarization tour introducing potential buyers to a destination or venue. First class premium seating and service in the front of the aircraft.

flag carrier The airline or carrier representing a country and serving international routes.

freight forwarder A shipping company.

frequent flyer Traveler who claims benefits from frequent travel on one carrier.

ground operator A vendor handling transfer from airport to hotel and other local transportation.

group travel When meeting participants all depart at the same time from the same departure city.

hospitality desk A desk or an office, staffed to service delegates during a meeting.

national tourist offices (NTOs) Organizations set to promote tourism to that destination.

overbook When an airline sells more seats than are available to offset the no-show factor.

passport A legal document permitting travel from one country to another.

professional congress organizer (PCO) Same as a meeting planner with extended services such as tours.

protocol Customs dealing with diplomacy, procedures, and etiquette.

right-to-work permit Official permission necessary to fill a professional position with one from outside the destination or country.

simultaneous translation Translation of one language into another while a speaker addresses an audience.

tour guides　Professional guides who accompany tours and explain history and points of interest.

value-added tax (VAT)　A tax imposed on the supply of goods and services by European Union (EU) countries.

VAT reclaim　A portion or all of the VAT reclaimed by those qualifying for tax exemption.

visa　An official document permitting entry into a country for a specific purpose.

Resources

Meeting Information

The following may be contacted for information on planning meetings:

Business-to-Business/Products and Services
Adams Business Media
68-860 Perez Road
Cathedral City, CA 92234
760-770-4370
760-770-2871 (Fax)
http://www.AdamsInteractive.com

Adams Business Media publishes five industry magazines and also has online information by specific topics. Inquire about its products and services, book mart, directories, reprint services, and site inspection register.

The Convention Center Guide
Gore & Osment Publications Pty, Ltd.
8 McLachlan Avenue
Rashcutters Bay
NSW 2011, Australia
612-9361 5244
612-9360 7558 (Fax)
http://www.jbfp.com.au/CCG/

This guide provides data about leading convention and exhibition centers and hotels with meeting facilities in the Asia–Pacific region.

Encyclopedia of Associations
Gale's Business Catalogue
Gale Research Inc.
835 Penobscot Building
Detroit, MI 48226-4094
1-800-877-GALE

313-961-6083
http://www.gale.com.

This provides a comprehensive list of associations. You may research specific associations that can provide you with niche information in specific areas. The directory lists associations by category, along with contact information.

GAVEL published by M&C (Meetings and Conventions)
REED Travel Group (Division of Reed Elsevier, Inc.)
500 Plaza Drive
Secaucus, NJ 07094-3626
201-902-2000
201-319-1796 (Fax)
http://www.tmd

This guide for planners provides lists of airlines, car rentals, and cruise lines, as well as a hotel directory outlining pertinent facility information.

The Guide to Campus, Non-Profit & Retreat Meeting Facilities
P.O. Box 279
164 Railroad, Suite 250
Minturn, CO 81645
1-800-933-3500
1-800-933-3534 (Fax)
http://vail.net/guide

This is a guide to alternate meeting facilities.

Local Convention and Visitors' Bureau
Call the local Convention and Visitors' Bureau (CVB) and request a current copy of its *Destination Planning Guide* or *Group Tour and Meeting Planners Directory* or any variation of its publication that lists city resources for meetings or conferences designed to assist planners.

MARRIOTT Meeting Planners Guide
MARRIOTT's Meeting Network
International Headquarters
MARRIOTT Drive
Washington, DC 20058
1-800-626-3614

Call the local Marriott sales office and request a copy of the guide, which is a directory of Marriott-owned facilities with hotel and meeting data (including diagrams of all conference rooms).

MPI Bookstore Catalog
Meeting Professionals International
1950 Stemmons Freeway, Suite 5018

Dallas, TX 75207-3109
214-712-7700
214-712-7770 (Fax)

The catalog lists meeting planner publications and resources.

Official Meeting Facilities Guide—North America
OMFG/Circulation Department
Reed Travel Group
500 Plaza Drive
Secaucus, NJ 07094-3626
1-800-446-6551 (Customer Service)
201-319-1761 (Fax)

This is a guide of meeting facilities outlining the location in a city, distance from airports, rates and amenities, and local attractions. Information about the listed facilities includes size of the rooms, number that may be accommodated, and setup.

Meeting Publications

The following magazines are available to those who plan meetings (call to receive a subscription):

Association Management
(Publication of American Society
    of Association Executives)
1575 I Street NW
Washington, DC 20005
202-626-2757

Association Meetings
Adams Business Media
60 Main Street
Maynard, MA 01754
978-897-5552
978-897-6824 (Fax)
http://www.meetingsnet.com

Convene
(Journal of the Professional Con-
    vention Management Associa-
    tion, or PCMA)
100 Vestavia, Suite 220
Birmingham, AL 35216-3742

205-823-7262
205-822-3891 (Fax)

Corporate & Incentive Travel
2600 N. Military Trail, 4th Floor
Boca Raton, FL 33431-6309
561-989-0600

Corporate Meetings & Incentives
Adams Business Media
60 Main Street
Maynard, MA 01754
978-897-5552
978-897-6824 (Fax)
http://www.meetingsnet.com

Exhibitor
206 S. Broadway, Suite 745
Rochester, MN 55904-6565
507-289-6556
507-289-5253 (Fax)
www.exhibitornet.com

Insurance Conference Planner
Adams Business Media
60 Main Street
Maynard, MA 01754
978-897-5552
978-897-6824 (Fax)
http://www.meetingsnet.com

Medical Meetings
Adams Business Media
60 Main Street
Maynard, MA 01754
978-897-5552
978-897-6824 (Fax)
http://www.meetingsnet.com

Meetings & Conventions
500 Plaza Drive
Secaucus, NJ 07094-3626
201-902-1700
201-319-1796 (Fax)
www.meetings-conventions.com

Meeting News
P.O. Box 1189
Skokie, IL 60076-8189
1-800-447-0138
847-647-5972 (Fax)
http://www.meetingnews.com

*Meetings Today/Business Travel
    News*
CMP Publications, Inc.

600 Community Drive
Manhasset, NY 11030
516-562-5000
www.cmpnet.com

Religious Conference Manager
Adams Business Media
60 Main Street
Maynard, MA 01754
978-897-5552
978-897-6824 (Fax)
http://www.meetingsnet.com

Successful Meetings
355 Park Avenue S.
New York, NY 10010
212-592-6403
212-592-6600 (Fax)
www.successmtgs.com

Technology Meetings
Adams Business Media
60 Main Street
Maynard, MA 01754
978-897-5552
978-897-6824 (Fax)
http://www.meetingsnet.com

Travel & Leisure
1120 Avenue of the Americas
New York, NY 10036
212-382-5600
212-382-5877 (Fax)
www.travel&leisure.com

Audiovisual Technology in Hotels

The following hotels offer new audiovisual technology:

* Hilton Hotels TeleSuite Network

Each suite is outfitted with a conference table for five. The conferees can see another group on a 92-inch screen via digital life-size real-time images, and the other group can see them. Each suite is a mirror image of the other. When live, it appears everyone is in one room around a conference table for ten.

- ITT Sheraton

GlobalVue videoconferencing system, in partnership with VueCom, will offer transmission over high-speed, fiber-optic lines.

- Marriott Hotels and Resorts

They offer videoconferencing capability, delivering television images to outlying units.

Audiovisual Technology On-Line

There is an increase in the number of hotels that provide videoconference rooms for virtual meetings conducted in different locations. Check out their locations at these on-line addresses:

Bedouk Online
A database of international hotels and conference centers
www.bedouk.com

Holiday Inn Conference Network
RFP and planning aid
www.confnet.holiday-inn.com

The Meeting Guide
International Association of Convention and Visitors' Bureaus
http://www.iacvb.org

PlanSoft
A database of hotels and convention centers
http://www.plansoft.com

International Meetings

For more information on planning international meetings, contact any of the following:

American Association of Language Specialists (AALS)
1000 Connecticut Avenue NW, Suite 9
Washington, DC 20036
301-986-1542

American Society for Industrial Security (ASIS)
1655 N. Ft. Myer Drive, Suite 1200
Arlington, VA 22209
703-522-5800
703-243-4954 (Fax)
(A security association)

American Translators Association
109 Croton Avenue
Ossining, NY 10562
914-941-1500
(*Translation Services Directory* available to nonmembers for fee)

American Translators Association (ATA)
1800 Diagonal Road, Suite 220
Alexandria, VA 22314
703-683-6100

ATA Carnet
U.S. Council for International Business
202-371-1316 (Washington, DC)
212-354-4480 (New York)

The Complete Guide to Executive Manners
by Letitia Baldridge
New York: Rawson Associates, 1985

EventPlanner
Country-by-Country Information
http://www.eventplanner.com/cities/europe/uk.htm

Culturgram Briefings
http://www.byu.edu/culturgrams

Foreign Languages for Travelers
http://www.travlang.com/languages

International Association of Convention and Visitors' Bureaus
http://www.iacvb.org

Meetings Industry Mall
http://www.mim.com

National Tourist Offices in the U.S. and Abroad
http://www.mbnet.mb.ca./lucas/travel/tourism-offices.html

Travelers' Advisories—U.S. State Department

http://www.stolaf.edu/network/travel-advisories.html

Travelers' Health—U.S. Centers for Disease Control
http://www.cdc.gov/travel/travel.html

Exchange Rates (current currency rates)
www.oanda.com

Fly Rights
U.S. Department of Transportation (DOT)
Consumer Affairs
400 7th Street SW, Room 10405
Washington, DC 20590
(Pamphlet listing rights of all passengers on aircraft)

Global Assist
202-783-7474
(American Express cardholders may call collect for emergencies that require a doctor, lawyer, banker, etc.)

International Association for Medical Assistance to Travelers
417 Center Street
Lewiston, NY 14092
716-754-4883

International Association of Convention and Visitors' Bureaus
217-359-8881
217-359-0965 (Fax)
www.iacvb.org

International Association of Professional Conference Organizers
3 Oxdoune Close
Stoke D'Abernon Cobham
Surrey KT111 2SZ

United Kingdom
011-44 372 843397
011-44 372 842002 (Fax)

International Association of Professional Congress Organizers (IAPCO)
40 Rue Washington
B-1050 Brussels, Belgium
011-32 640 7106
011-32 640 4731 (Fax)
www.iapco.org

International Congress & Convention Association (ICCA)
Entrada 121/122 1096EB
Amsterdam, The Netherlands
011-31 30 690 1171
011-31 20 600 0781 (Fax)
www.congress city.com/icca

International Trade Administration (ITA)
U.S. Department of Commerce
Office of Public Affairs
14th and Constitution Avenue NW, Room 4805
Washington, DC 20230
202-377-3808
(For Americans doing business abroad)

Meridian VAT Reclaim, Inc.
125 West 55th Street, 8th floor
New York, NY 10019
212-554-6600
212-974-0673 (Fax)

Overcoming Jet Lag
by Charles Ehre and Lynn Waller Scanlon
New York: Berkeley Books, 1983

R.P. Werth & Associates, Inc.
1313 Sawyer Bend Circle

Franklin, TN 37069
615-377-3200
615-377-3666 (Fax)
(A security firm)

SOS International
8 Neshaminy Interplex, Suite 207
Trevose, PA 19053
215-244-1500
215-244-9617 (Fax)
(A security firm)

Trade Information Center
U.S. Department of Commerce
International Trade Administration
1-800-USA TRADE

U.S. Department of Commerce
Desk Officer (specify country)
14th and Constitution Avenue NW
Washington, DC 20230
202-377-2000
(Trade show information)

U.S. Embassies
travel.state.gov/links.html

U.S. State Department
21st and C Street NW, Room 4800
Washington, DC 20520
202-647-5225
http://www.travel.state.gov
(Travel advisory hot line)

U.S. State Department
Any U.S. Embassy or Consulate
202-647-4000

U.S. State Department
Citizens Emergency Center
202-647-4000

Meeting Associations

American Hotel & Motel Association (AH&MA)
1201 New York Avenue NW, Suite 600
Washington, DC 20005
202-289-3100
202-289-3199 (Fax)
http://www.ahma.com

American Management Association (AMA)
1601 Broadway
New York, NY 10019-7420
212-586-8100
http://www.amanet.org

American Society for Training and Development (ASTD)
1630 Duke Street, P.O. Box 1443
Alexandria, VA 22313
703-638-8100
703-683-1523 (Fax)
www.astd.org

American Society of Association Executives (ASAE)
1575 Eye Street, NW
Washington, DC 20005
202-626-2757
www.plansoft.com

American Society of Travel Agents (The) (ASTA)
1101 King Street
Alexandria, VA 22314
703-739-2782
703-684-8319 (Fax)
www.astnet.com

Association for Convention Operations Management (ACOM)
1819 Peachtree Street, NE, Suite 560
Atlanta, GA 30309
404-351-3220
404-351-3348 (Fax)

Convention Liaison Council (CLC)
1575 Eye Street, NW
Washington, DC 20005
202-626-2764
202-371-8825 (Fax)

Exposition Service Contractors Association (ESCA)*
Union Station, Suite 210
400 S. Houston Street
Dallas, Texas 75202
214-742-9217
214-741-2519 (Fax)
www.esca.org

Healthcare Convention & Exhibitors Association (HCEA)
5775 Peachtree Dunwoody Road, Suite 5000G
Atlanta, GA 30342
404-252-3663
404-252-0774 (Fax)

Hotel Sales & Marketing Association International (HSMAI)
1300 L Street NW, Suite 1020
Washington, DC 20005
202-789-0089
202-789-1725 (Fax)
www.hsmai.org

*ESCA & IAEM collaborated to produce the *Annual Guide to Exposition Service* as a service to exposition managers, association executives, meeting planners, exhibit managers and others involved in the trade show and exposition industry.

International Association of Auditorium Managers (IAAM)
4425 West Airport Freeway, Suite 590
Irving, TX 75062
214-255-8020
214-255-9582 (Fax)

International Association of Conference Centers (IACC)
243 N. Lindbergh Boulevard
St. Louis, MO 63141
314-993-8575
314-993-8919 (Fax)
www.IACConline.com

International Association of Convention and Visitor Bureaus (IACVB)
2000 L Street NW, #702
Washington, DC 20036
202-296-7888
202-296-7889 (Fax)
www.iacvb.org

International Association of Exposition Managers (IAEM)*
719 Indiana Avenue
Indianapolis, IN 46202
317-NET-NAEM (638-6236)
317-687-0017 (Fax)

International Association of Festivals (IAFE)
P.O. Box 985
Springfield, MO 65801
417-862-5771
417-862-0156 (Fax)

International Association of Professional Congress Organizers (IAPCO)
(32) 2 640-71-05

International Congress & Convention Association (ICCA)
(31) 20-690-1171

International Special Events Society (ISES)
9202 N. Meridian Street, Suite 200
Indianapolis, IN 46260
317-571-5601
317-571-5603 (Fax)

Meeting Professionals International (MPI)
4455 LBJ Freeway, Suite 1200
Dallas, TX 75244-5903
972-702-3000
972-702-3070 (Fax)
http://www.mpiweb.org

National Speakers Association (NSA)
1500 South Priest Drive
Tempe, AZ 85281
602-968-2552
602-968-0911 (Fax)

Professional Convention Management Association (PCMA)
100 Vestavia, Suite 220
Birmingham, AL 35216-3742
205-823-7262
205-822-3891 (Fax)

Society of Corporate Meeting Professionals (SCMP)
1819 Peachtree Road, NE, Suite 620
Atlanta, GA 30309
404-355-9932
404-351-3348 (Fax)

*Ibid.

Society of Incentive & Travel Executives (SITE)
21 West 38th Street, 10th Floor
New York, NY 10018
212-575-0910
212-575-1838 (Fax)
www.site@ix.netcom.org

Trade Show Exhibitors Association
5502 Backlick Road, Suite 105
Springfield, VA 22151
703-941-3725
703-941-8275 (Fax)
E-mail: tsea@tsea.org

Index